Salvation Isn't Free... It's Been Paid For!

or,

What to do With Purple Bunnies

by

James Prest

TEACH Services, Inc.
www.TEACHServices.com

World rights reserved. This book or any portion thereof may not be copied or reproduced in any form or manner whatever, except as provided by law, without the written permission of the publisher, except by a reviewer who may quote brief passages in a review.

This book was written to provide truthful information in regard to the subject matter covered. The author assumes full responsibility for the accuracy of all facts and quotations as cited in this book. The opinions expressed in this book are the author's personal views and interpretation of the Bible, Spirit of Prophecy, and/or contemporary authors and do not necessarily reflect those of TEACH Services, Inc.

This book is sold with the understanding that the publisher is not engaged in giving spiritual, legal, medical, or other professional advice. If authoritative advice is needed, the reader should seek the counsel of a competent professional

Copyright © 2011 TEACH Services, Inc.
ISBN-13:978-1-57258-658-1 (Paperback)
978-1-57258-659-8 (Hardback)
978-1-57258-660-4 (E-book)
Library of Congress Control Number: 2011926739

Unless otherwise noted, all scripture is quoted from the King James Version. In addition, all scripture that is italicized was added as emphasis by the author.

Published by
TEACH Services, Inc.
www.TEACHServices.com

Dedication

This book is dedicated to those who love purple bunnies, those who think they do, those who are not sure if they do, and those who hate them with the bitterest passion.

Table of Contents

Dedication iii

Acknowledgments... vii

Chapter 1   "The love of the truth" 1

Chapter 2   "He spake, and it was done" 30

Chapter 3   "Speak the word only" 36

Chapter 4   "God spake all these words" 47

Chapter 5   "I the LORD have created it" 51

Chapter 6   "Kept by the power of God" 55

Chapter 7   "If he trust to his own righteousness" 59

Chapter 8   "Clean through the word" 65

Chapter 9   "By every word of God" 68

Chapter 10 "Taken in the devices" 78

Chapter 11 "What to do with purple bunnies" 87

Chapter 12 "Are you ready?" 98

Acknowledgments

O give thanks unto the LORD; for he is good:
for his mercy endureth for ever.

O give thanks unto the God of gods:
for his mercy endureth for ever.

O give thanks to the Lord of lords:
for his mercy endureth for ever.

To him who alone doeth great wonders:
for his mercy endureth for ever.

To him that by wisdom made the heavens:
for his mercy endureth for ever.

To him that stretched out the earth above the waters:
for his mercy endureth for ever.

To him that made great lights:
for his mercy endureth for ever:

The sun to rule by day:
for his mercy endureth for ever

The moon and stars to rule by night:
for his mercy endureth for ever.

To him that smote Egypt in their firstborn:
for his mercy endureth for ever:

And brought out Israel from among them:
for his mercy endureth for ever:

With a strong hand, and with a stretched out arm:
for his mercy endureth for ever.

To him which divided the Red sea into parts:
for his mercy endureth for ever:

And made Israel to pass through the midst of it:
for his mercy endureth for ever:

But overthrew Pharaoh and his host in the Red sea:
for his mercy endureth for ever.

To him which led his people through the wilderness:
for his mercy endureth for ever.

To him which smote great kings:
for his mercy endureth for ever:

And slew famous kings:
for his mercy endureth for ever:

Sihon king of the Amorites:
for his mercy endureth for ever:

And Og the king of Bashan:
for his mercy endureth for ever:

And gave their land for an heritage:
for his mercy endureth for ever:

Even an heritage unto Israel his servant:
for his mercy endureth for ever.

Who remembered us in our low estate:
for his mercy endureth for ever:

And hath redeemed us from our enemies:
for his mercy endureth for ever.

Who giveth food to all flesh:
for his mercy endureth for ever.

O give thanks unto the God of heaven:
for his mercy endureth for ever.

(Psalm 136)

    I want to give thanks to my mother, Evelyn Crouse, for being a loving mom. Thanks to Miss Ricky for being my friend and for caring so much. Thanks to Ace Hedger, who has given me deeper insights concerning "the machine." Thanks to Kalie Kelch for being patient and working so hard with me in editing this book. And thanks also to all of my supportive friends who have helped and encouraged me in my work.

"In matters of conscience the soul must be left untrammeled. No one is to control another's mind, to judge for another, or to prescribe his duty. God gives to every soul freedom to think, and to follow his own convictions. 'Every one of us shall give account of himself to God.' No one has a right to merge his own individuality in that of another. In all matters where principle is involved, 'let every man be fully persuaded in his own mind.' Romans 14:12, 5."

~ *Desire of Ages*, p. 550

Chapter 1

"The love of the truth"

2 Thessalonians 2:10

Are you ready?

"Hear the word of the LORD . . . My people are destroyed for lack of knowledge: because thou hast *rejected* knowledge, I will also reject thee" (Hosea 4:1, 6).

"This is the condemnation, that light is come into the world, and men loved darkness rather than light, because their deeds were evil" (John 3:19). Every soul possesses the power to reason and has the choice to either love the light of truth or the darkness of error—whether he will accept or reject the knowledge that God gives. No one is forced to love falsehoods; it is a conscious choice to be made by the thinking individual. The choice to either love truth or error is an action performed by the mind. It is separate from the emotions and feelings. There is no internal default set in man that forces him to love lies. In the end, when "God shall bring every work into judgment, with every secret thing, whether it be good, or whether it be evil" (Eccl. 12:14), men will be condemned because they chose to love lies rather than truth.

"And with all deceivableness of unrighteousness in them that perish; because they received not the love of the truth, that they might be saved. And for this cause God shall send them strong delusion, that they should believe a lie: That they all might be damned who believed not the truth, but had pleasure in unrighteousness" (2 Thess. 2:10-12).

It is not any arbitrary act on the part of God that causes Him to send strong delusions to men. Man, the free moral agent, has the choice to either love truth or error, and when men don't receive the love of the truth, God, acting only according to the choice of man himself, allows strong delusions to overtake them.

Jesus said, "If I had not come and spoken unto them, they had not had sin: but now they have no cloak for their sin" (John 15:22). When truth is presented to the mind, or even the opportunity to hear truth, when men shut their eyes and close their ears, "lest at any time they should see with their eyes and hear with their ears, and should understand with their heart" (Matt. 13:15), they are placing themselves under condemnation. They can have no excuse, no cloak for their mistakes and misunderstandings, for truth was freely given them either to hate or to love, and by shutting their eyes, closing their ears, and turning their head, they make a decision that will bring its sure results.

"And ye shall know the truth, and the truth shall make you free" (John 8:32). These words are full of hope and instruction. Falsehoods are what bind men down in misery. Should the beauty of truth shine upon every soul in all its glorious luster, and that truth be accepted into the heart, there would be nothing that could bring men down from living as if in the atmosphere of heaven. God is good, and could all the deceptive falsehoods be removed concerning His character, man would be a possessor of an endless peace. Satan, however, would not have this.

But what is a lie? A lie is something that makes truth appear like what it is not. When something is lied about, in reality the thing that was lied about really exists. But that thing which the lie sought to

Chapter 1 — "The love of the truth"

establish, in reality does not exist, *except in the minds of those who believe the lie*. Lies exist because there are such things as lies, but if the things that the lies are seeking to establish do not exist, shall we allow them to affect our lives? Satan has lied about the character of God. In reality, the character of God exists in its beauty, but that which the lies of Satan seek to establish, in reality, do not exist, *except in the minds of those who believe his lies*. It is because men choose to love things that aren't real that they are so miserable. In the day of final judgment, men will be lost because they chose to love things that didn't really exist and because they chose to hate those things that did.

But how can we find out for sure what is truth? The different expressed views of what is right are various and discordant, so how then shall we know for ourselves what is truth?

Jesus said, "My doctrine is not mine, but his that sent me. If any man will do his will, he shall know of the doctrine, whether it be of God, or whether I speak of myself" (John 7:16, 17). Full of significance are these words that come to us straight from the Son of God. Here Christ unmistakably outlines what exactly man must do to come to a knowledge of truth. "*If any man will do his will*, he shall know of the doctrine." But what is the doctrine? Jesus does not say. The only thing He says is how to come to a knowledge of it. "If any man will do his will." This is the requirement.

Should the truth of heaven be found out to be something other than what you thought it was, would you do the will of God by accepting the light given and live your life accordingly? Or, would you resist the light, insisting that it cannot be correct because it does not line up with your ideas of truth? If you are not willing to accept the truth that God may give, and be willing to live by it, then there is no hope in the words of Christ that you shall ever come to a knowledge of truth. Jesus gives no exceptions. Will you know of the doctrine? Jesus answers, "If any man will do his will, *he shall know of the doctrine.*"

God forces no man to believe truth anymore than He forces them to accept a lie. There is no reason to fear that upon studying a certain Bible topic that you will be forced into believing error if you open yourself up to something that cuts across your established views of truth. Jesus says plainly that if a man is willing to do God's will, he shall know what true doctrine is. He said also that the Holy Spirit "will guide you into all truth" (John 16:13). We can therefore rest safe in these words of the One who died for us. We should never be afraid of searching the Scriptures, for God has given them to us that we might not be afraid. "And ye shall seek me, and find me, when ye shall search for me with all your heart. And I will be found of you, saith the LORD" (Jer. 29:13, 14).

When studying the Scriptures it is crucial to put all of our ideas of truth aside, to put them *all* on the shelf, and study the Scriptures in the light of the Scriptures, and not in the light of our established opinions. There is no internal or external force exhibited that can keep you from picking back up again those cherished views of truth and holding them oh so close to your heart. You are free to believe whatever you will. But the requirement that Jesus gave in order for you to come to a knowledge of true doctrine is that you be willing to accept the light that He may give. "He that trusteth in his own heart is a fool: but whoso walketh wisely, he shall be delivered" (Prov. 28:26).

"Thus saith the LORD; Cursed be the man that trusteth in man, and maketh flesh his arm" (Jer. 17:5). Oh how many there are who hear the words of man and accept them as truth without first searching the Scriptures to see whether or not the things that they have heard are so (Act 17:11). They trust in man, and a curse is pronounced upon them. They have failed to follow the instruction of Paul, *"Prove all things*; hold fast that which is good" (1 Thess. 5:21). Because it is

Chapter 1 — "The love of the truth"

easier to do so, many hold fast to the words of men as that which is good, before they have first proved them, before they have first tested them by the words of Scripture to determine whether or not they are true. Thus thousands are led into believing and loving midnight error.

Christ gives us the following instruction: "Take heed therefore *how* ye hear" (Luke 8:18). How we hear a message that comes to us more often than not determines what we will do with it. It is not so much *what* we hear, but *how* we hear it. We are to listen with a sincere desire to know what is truth and to do it, asking the Lord to lead and guide our understanding and to keep us from rising up against truth that, in our blindness, we personally detect as error. Then we are to "search the Scriptures" (John 5:39) to "prove all things," and *then* we are to "hold fast that which is good" (1 Thess. 5:21). Not the bad, but the good only. King Solomon said, "The simple [foolish] believeth *every word*: but the prudent man looketh well to his going" (Prov. 14:15). And John warns, "Believe not every spirit, but try the spirits whether they are of God: because many false prophets are gone out into the world" (1 John 4:1).

> *Because it is easier to do so, many hold fast to the words of men as that which is good, before they have first proved them, before they have first tested them by the words of Scripture to determine whether or not they are true.*

The spirit with which we are to enter the study of the Scriptures is well described in the book of Job. "That which I see not teach thou me: if I have done iniquity, I will do no more" (Job 34:32). Those who come to the study of God's Word with a self-sufficient attitude cannot expect the aid of the Holy Spirit. Self-sufficiency feels no need of help and therefore has no desire to receive it. The attitude with which we come to the Scriptures determines whether or not the Holy Spirit will guide our understanding.

While many of the things that men say are true, it is fatal to the salvation of the soul to believe the truth because man has said it. Man's word is not our foundation. The foundation that we are to build our knowledge of truth upon is the Word of God. This is the only sure foundation. "Whosoever heareth these sayings of mine, and doeth them," says Jesus, "I will liken him unto a wise man" (Matt. 7:24) "which built an house, and digged deep, and laid the foundation on a rock" (Luke 6:48). "And the rain descended, and the floods came, and the winds blew, and beat upon that house; and it fell not: for it was founded upon a rock. And every one that heareth these sayings of mine, and doeth them not, shall be likened unto a foolish man, which built his house upon the sand: And the rain descended, and the floods came, and the winds blew, and beat upon that house; and it fell: and great was the fall of it" (Matt. 7:25-27).

When the trials come, those who have based their knowledge of truth on the Word of God *alone*, who have dug deep into the Scriptures and know for themselves what is truth, they shall not fall, for they have built upon the rock. They will know that their position is correct because they have familiarized themselves with the truth and have grounded themselves in it. They have become identified with the truth, with the rock that will stand the fiercest tempest. They know that their position is sustained by the Word of God, and they will not be moved by the storm.

But those who are content to accept truth from human pen or lips, however pure that truth may be, will not stand when the storms of opposition come. They will be shaken by the fierce winds and be

Chapter 1 — "The love of the truth"

carried away by the floods. Then they will see that they have not known the truth for themselves. They will realize that their knowledge of what they thought to be truth has been based on what, so often, misinformed man has told them. They have no foundation, no roots to hold them in place. They have built their house on the sandy sayings of men, and with those sands they will be taken away without a trace. The only thing left after the storm will be the lone rock, which they neglected to build upon. Thus the words of the Lord will stand true: "Cursed be the man that trusteth in man, and maketh flesh his arm" (Jer. 17:5).

Overwhelming multitudes of people accept or reject a message purely based on the messenger or who supports his message. We must not judge the man, but the message. Many have rejected the light and warnings of heaven because of their prejudices toward the messenger. But God would have us accept the truth upon its own merit. He would not have us swayed by opinion or influence. Should every soul on earth except for the most extreme fanatics reject a truth, however small and seemingly unimportant that truth may be, God demands of us that we stand by that truth, though all the world pronounce us as fools.

"For seven years a man continued to go up and down the streets of Jerusalem, declaring the woes that were to come upon the city. By day and by night he chanted the wild dirge: 'A voice from the east! a voice from the west! a voice from the four winds! a voice against Jerusalem and against the temple! a voice against the bridegrooms and the brides! a voice against the whole people!'—[Milman, *The History of the Jews*, book 13]. This strange being was imprisoned and scourged, but no complaint escaped his lips. To insult and abuse he answered only: 'Woe, woe to Jerusalem!' 'woe, woe to the inhabitants thereof!' His warning cry ceased not until he was slain in the siege he had foretold" (Ellen G. White, *The Great Controversy*, p. 30).

Salvation Isn't Free... It's Been Paid For!

There were many who hated this messenger and rejected his message. They thought that he was nothing more than a mad fool who was utterly deceived. And, oh how terrible were the results of rejecting the fanatic's warning of impending doom! He had spoken truth, but blind prejudice, gross error, and the love of a lie kept the masses from escaping fearful destruction. And how many times has the same thing happened again and again, on a lesser or larger scale? Thus we have the two dangers: rejecting what man says and accepting what man says.

"Trust in the LORD with all thine heart; and lean not unto thine own understanding. In all thy ways acknowledge him, and he shall direct thy paths. Be not wise in thine own eyes: fear the LORD, and depart from evil" (Prov. 3:5-7). This is man's only safety—trusting in God. The One who "cannot lie," "the faithful and true witness," He is the one that we can safely trust (Titus 1:2; Rev. 3:14). But if we will not hear His words, if we will not open our eyes, if we choose to turn our heads in another direction and refuse to hear His voice, we can have no safety. If we have no time to study and to learn what is truth, if the cares and pleasures of this world are allowed to absorb all of our attention so that we have no time to search the Scriptures and to determine truth from error, then we will be left prey to the deceptions of the wicked one. The Word of God is within our reach, and the Holy Spirit is at hand to teach, and if we are deceived unto our own condemnation, it is no ones fault but our own.

The vital key to trusting in the Lord is to trust in Him *alone*. Man cannot be trusted, and that includes ourselves. "Lean not unto *thine own understanding*" is the instruction given us of heaven (Prov. 3:5). Solomon went on to say, "There is a way which *seemeth* right unto a man, but the end thereof are the ways of death" (Prov. 14:12). God means what He says. It is not our place to take a text of Scripture

Chapter 1 — "The love of the truth"

and twist it to make it mean what we want it to mean. The apostle Peter speaks of this class as those who "wrest" the Scriptures "unto their own destruction" (2 Peter 3:16). It is the duty of all to determine for themselves what the Lord is communicating to them through His Word. But leaning on our own understanding and twisting the words of truth to our own destruction is just what the devil would have us do. It is far wiser to leave a difficult text of Scripture alone and come back to it later than to cast your own interpretation upon the words of truth.

In his letter to Timothy, Paul brought out the fact that there are such things as the "doctrines of devils" (1 Tim. 4:1). The minions of evil have no purpose of good to accomplish by their teachings. They are bent only in the utter misery and destruction of the human race. The longer and more painful the torture they can inflict upon mind and body, the greater their hellish glee. If men will accept scriptural interpretation from no one but the Holy Spirit, they shall be safe. Christ promised that the Spirit of truth, "will guide you into all truth," and "shall teach you all things" (John 16:13; 14:26). This is our safety, depending upon the Author of the Book to interpret it to us.

Although we are to rely on the Holy Spirit to guide us into all truth, the Lord has a place in His work for teachers. "God hath set some in the church, first apostles, secondarily prophets, thirdly teachers" (1 Cor. 12:28). It is not evil for man to teach the Word of God. The problem is when the student accepts what the teacher says without first proving the interpretation for himself to see if it stands up to the test and is in harmony with the rest of the Scriptures. What if the teacher is deceived as to what is truth? How will the student know unless he first discovers for himself what is truth? "The simple believeth every word: but the prudent man looketh well to his going" (Prov. 14:15).

John, writing to those who knew the truth after having warned them of false teachers, said, *"ye need not that any man teach you*: but as the same anointing teacheth you of all things, and is truth, and is no lie, and even as it hath taught you, ye shall abide in him" (1 John 2:27). Teachers are not necessary for man to come to an understanding of the truths contained in the Scriptures. The Holy Spirit alone is sufficient. If the Spirit of truth was not sufficient for man to come to a knowledge of truth, then he would be forced into risking his own happiness and salvation upon the word of another man, only daring to hope that he would not be led astray.

Large is the class of people who insist that what an elder or minister says is to be respected because of his age and experience in the Word. They will quote to the youth all the Bible verses that show that this is what God would have them do. But how many forget to show the youth those crucial texts that reveal truths which cannot be safely forgotten. For example, look at the following three texts: "Great men are not always wise: neither do the aged understand judgment" (Job 32:9). "Now the end of the commandment is charity out of a pure heart, and of a good conscience, and of faith unfeigned: From which some having swerved have turned aside unto vain jangling; Desiring to be teachers of the law; understanding neither what they say, nor whereof they affirm" (1 Tim. 1:5-7). "The time will come when they will not endure sound doctrine; but after their own lusts shall they heap to themselves teachers, having itching ears; And they shall turn away their ears from the truth, and shall be turned unto fables" (2 Tim. 4:3, 4).

An aged man with experience in the Scriptures, a minister in

Chapter 1 — "The love of the truth"

the pulpit, may be nothing more than an old and experienced fool who has done nothing more but learn well how to twist the words of God, present them in such a way as to support his own theories and opinions, cast a favorable light upon them, and then feed them to a captive audience who will not do so much as even question him. But how are we to know what is truth? How are we to know whether or not these teachers are teaching the truth? They are to be tested by the Word of God.

Allow no man to control your mind by letting them tell you what truth is and what you must believe. This is Satan's method of controlling the minds of his prey, but Christ's method of teaching is of an entirely different character. When Christ was asked, "What shall I do to inherit eternal life?" He answered, "What is written in the law? how readest thou?" (Luke 10:25, 26). Christ did not force truth upon the lawyer. He left him open to believe whatever he would. *"How readest thou?"* He asked. Anyone who seeks to manipulate another into believing as he does is a successful agent of Satan, for whether he compels his prey to believe a lie or even the truth, the foundation will not, it cannot, be upon the Word of God. It will be based solely and only upon the word of man, and such a foundation will give way when the storm comes.

This is not to say that when a preacher or teacher of the Word presents truth that he should be dwindling and uncertain as to what he is presenting. Jesus did not teach this way. When He was done speaking "the people were astonished at his doctrine: For he taught them as one having authority, and not as the scribes" (Matt. 7:28, 29). Preachers and teachers of the Word of God must be clear and concise, but never guilt the conscience into believing a certain way. This is to be the rule. They are to allow their listeners to be free to accept or reject what is taught. Pressuring them to accept what is taught does not leave their minds free to think, reason, and choose for themselves. It is manipulative. And even though the listener is not forced into believing anything, by manipulating them to believe as they do, they are trying to act as their conscience. The Lord of heaven commands us saying, "Let every man be fully persuaded in his own mind" (Rom. 14:5).

The Jews of old sought to compel the consciences of those over whom they held influence. There was a certain blind man to whom Jesus had restored sight. "But the Jews did not believe concerning him, that he had been blind, and received his sight, until they called the parents of him that had received his sight. And they asked them, saying, Is this your son, who ye say was born blind? how then doth he now see? His parents answered them and said, We know that this is our son, and that he was born blind: But by what means he now seeth, we know not; or who hath opened his eyes, we know not: he is of age; ask him: he shall speak for himself. These words spake his parents, *because they feared the Jews*: for the Jews had agreed already, that if any man did confess that he was Christ, he should be put out of the synagogue. Therefore said his parents, He is of age; ask him" (John 9:18-23).

From this incidence recorded in the Scriptures, we see the craftiness of those who manipulate others into believing as they do. The parents of the blind man dared not confess that Christ had healed their son because they would be put out of the synagogue. And do not many churches of today do the same? Alas, some churches will remove your name from their books if you do not agree with all of their doctrines or if you believe one that they do not agree with. But a name in a church book means nothing. As long as the name of the individual is "written in the Lamb's book of life," let men do whatever they will to the individual's record (Rev. 21:27).

These parents were brought to a position where they had to either

Chapter 1 — "The love of the truth"

confess or deny Christ, and the wicked, mind-controlling system of those who would crucify the Lord of glory led the parents into denying Him. "Whosoever therefore shall confess me before men, him will I confess also before my Father which is in heaven. But whosoever shall deny me before men, him will I also deny before my Father which is in heaven" (Matt. 10:32, 33). A solemn denunciation is pronounced upon these mind-controlling servants of Satan—a denunciation that will not be undone unless they repent—"Woe unto you, scribes and Pharisees, hypocrites! for ye shut up the kingdom of heaven against men: for ye neither go in yourselves, neither suffer ye them that are entering to go in" (Matt. 23:13; see also Luke 11:52).

The mind-controlling principles of wickedness, which are conducive to sin, are often present in today's educational systems. "This is life eternal, that they might know thee the only true God, and Jesus Christ, whom thou hast sent" (John 17:3). Eternal life is to know God. This is the object of all true education. "He that loveth not knoweth not God; for God is love" (1 John 4:8). Since he that does not love does not know God, we must then conclude that to know God is to love Him. Eternal life is to know God; it is to love Him. "This is the love of God, that we keep his commandments" (1 John 5:3). Anything that fails of reaching this mark fails to reach the mark of all true education—man's salvation. The education that is not conducive to salvation and to the keeping of God's commandments, but that rather fosters sin and a love for it, cannot be a true education. True education is conducive to righteousness. False education is conducive to sin.

> *True education is conducive to righteousness. False education is conducive to sin*

Salvation Isn't Free... It's Been Paid For!

Preachers and Bible teachers are not infallible; they are not God. Man does not have the right to decide for another what is and what is not a right answer to a doctrinal question. The Word of God alone should be every student's guide as to what is truth. Preachers and teachers who try to stand in the place of God to tell an individual what is and what is not truth will have to answer to God for their actions.

One evil that to all appearances seems to be among the most innocent is when the student of the Word studies the Bible in such a way as to show himself approved to man. Many students study the Word of God so that when the test comes they can show themselves approved to their teachers. The Scriptures faithfully outline the students' duty in this matter: "Study to shew thyself *approved unto God*, a workman that needeth not to be ashamed, rightly dividing the word of truth" (2 Tim. 2:15). Preachers, teachers, parents, and friends are not infallible; they are not God. And who is man, that he has the right to decide for another what is and what is not a right answer to a doctrinal question? "If any man think that he knoweth any thing, he knoweth nothing yet as he ought to know" (1 Cor. 8:2).

When men seek to manipulate others into believing as they do, they seek to take away the ability of others to think and reason for themselves. The method of testing and grading, causing the student to show himself approved unto man, is just as surely mind control as telling someone what they are to believe, only this method is more indirect because it uses less force. But nevertheless, it is still manipulative to the end that the student may be programmed to believe whatever his instructor teaches him. This type of mind control is imperceptibly sly—it doesn't appear dangerous, but it is, therefore, to be shunned all the more. Those who involve themselves in this type of instruction are guilty of controlling the minds of those who are weaker than they are. And who is man to take away the ability of

Chapter 1 — "The love of the truth"

another person to think and reason for himself?

We are to share what we know, to share those things that have helped us, but we are not to manipulate another into believing as we do. We are to share what we know and then let them study, think, and reason for themselves to determine whether or not what we have told them is true. Should they accept what we say at our word, even if that something is true, their foundation will not withstand the storm. Our words, however pure and truthful, are not their foundation. We must show them that they need to build upon the Rock themselves.

When students must study in such a way as to give the correct answer that their instructor wants to hear, they cannot study to find and know truth for themselves, for if they do, they will lose the precious time needed to study and will not necessarily pass the test by giving the pre-prescribed answers of the teacher. The students are thus forced, by time and circumstances, to be nothing more than a mere replica of their teacher and the ideas of the authors of their textbooks. However deceived the teacher may be is how deceived his or her students will be. They cannot surpass their teacher's knowledge because they don't have time to learn things for themselves.

Instead of placing so much importance on the teacher's "right" answer, students should be left free to study and test things by the Word of God. That way the student will have a true foundation that will withstand the most terrible of storms, and this cannot be had when the student is limited by time and controlled by the materials presented by the teacher and textbooks. "Search the scriptures; for in them ye think ye have eternal life" (John 5:39).

Knowledge is its own reward. Regardless of how difficult it may seem to fight for truth, even when it goes against set practices and traditions, as students of the Word of God, one must stand firm. Even if it means getting a lower grade, failing a test, or doing poorly in a class, students should stand firm for what is written in the Scriptures and not simply write down the pre-prescribed answer they have been told to memorize.

There are those students who would give the answer that the teacher wants to hear and would do it in such a way so as to not technically deny what they believe to be the truth, but in reality, it is a denial of truth. The truth can be presented in such a way as to be misleading in its conclusion, but one must show our colors faithfully and unmistakably. In the moment of inspection, unless the truth is clearly confessed, it is denied, and this one cannot afford to do.

The true Christian's way of dealing with differences of scriptural understanding is found in the Word of God. "Come now, and let us reason together, saith the LORD" (Isa. 1:18). Those who use the principles of mind control will have nothing to do with coming together to reason anything, except as they see that they might be able, by skill and comeliness, to find a way to gently manipulate another's mind into believing as they do. There are many who do this without recognizing it as a bad thing because it was done to them. They see no harm in mind control and taking away the ability of others to think and reason for themselves. They are not even aware of the fact that they are involved in such a thing. They themselves have been deceived by the scheme, and they must also be brought out of the system of sin.

How sad it is when a student who is seeking truth and speaks his mind as to what he understands to be truth receives only critical remarks and put downs in response. Whether the most plain, blunt, and harrowing, or the most imperceptibly sly, the damaging comments many times roll in one after the other from both the teacher and the student's peers. But who will criticize a student of the Word? What person has the right to exercise the manipulative mind-controlling principles of Satan upon a searching child of God? When the day

Chapter 1 — "The love of the truth"

comes, the King of heaven shall say unto them, "Verily I say unto you, Inasmuch as ye have done it unto one of the least of these . . . ye have done it unto me" (Matt. 25:40).

What soul-searching words are these! And oh how far reaching! Many principals, instructors, and staff members, in general, have looked upon their students with suspicion, keeping a watchful eye on them as if waiting for them to do what is wrong. And how does this affect the character of the students? The students know they are not trusted, and they are led to feel that they are looked upon as little more than immoral individuals. Even the good things they do, they may feel that they must do in secret, lest they be caught and punished with the charge of breaking some God-given principle that God has not necessarily given nor of which they are guilty of breaking. And this doing of good things in secret, proves itself a great source of temptation to the unsuspecting youth. Thus the students once again are manipulated into doing things that they otherwise would not do. They are led into disregarding the instruction to "abstain from all appearance of evil" (1 Thess. 5:22). And when they are caught doing good deeds, they are rebuked for breaking this very instruction by the ones who set them up to break it through their evil surmising. Thus many students give up trying to seek the truth, and they succumb to the stereotype that is placed upon them that they are of little value and cannot do anything right.

"The wise educator, in dealing with his pupils, will seek to encourage confidence and to strengthen the sense of honor. Children and youth are benefited by being trusted. Many, even of the little children, have a high sense of honor; all desire to be treated with confidence and respect, and this is their right. They should not be led to feel that they cannot go out or come in without being watched. *Suspicion demoralizes, producing the very evils it seeks to prevent.*

Instead of watching continually, as if suspecting evil, teachers who are in touch with their pupils will discern the workings of the restless mind, and will set to work influences that will counteract evil. Lead the youth to feel that they are trusted, and there are few who will not seek to prove themselves worthy of the trust.

"On the same principle it is better to request than to command; the one thus addressed has opportunity to prove himself loyal to right principles. His obedience is the result of choice rather than compulsion" (Ellen G. White, *Education*, pp. 289, 290).

The wicked assumptions, foundationless speculations, and evil surmising have only the tendency to destroy both the predator and the prey. And Jesus still stands, speaking to the false teachers of the Scriptures these probing words: "Inasmuch as ye have done it unto one of the least of these . . . ye have done it unto me" (Matt. 25:40).

Christ said, "Why beholdest thou the mote that is in thy brother's eye, but perceivest not the beam that is in thine own eye?" (Luke 6:41). "Or how wilt thou say to thy brother, Let me pull out the mote out of thine eye; and, behold, a beam is in thine own eye? Thou hypocrite, first cast out the beam out of thine own eye; and then shalt thou see clearly to cast out the mote out of thy brother's eye" (Matt. 7:4, 5). How many times are these words rehearsed but are violated by the people who teach them? To these individuals, Jesus plainly says, "Judge not, that ye be not judged. For with what judgment ye judge, ye shall be judged: and with what measure ye mete, it shall be measured to you again" (Matt. 7:1, 2). "He that is without sin among you, let him first cast a stone" (John 8:7).

It matters not what reasons men may give to justify their evil surmising: "For God shall bring *every work* into judgment, with every secret thing, whether it be good, or whether it be evil." (Eccl. 12:14). "We must all appear before the judgment seat of Christ; that every

Chapter 1 — "The love of the truth"

one may receive the things done in his body, according to that he hath done, whether it be good or bad" (2 Cor. 5:10). There is no escaping this judgment. Jesus says, "The word that I have spoken, the same shall judge him in the last day" (John 12:48). Jesus is no liar. Teachers must trust their students and treat them like Christ would treat them, else condemnation come upon them that cannot be undone. While we are to be "wise as serpents," we are at the same time to be "harmless as doves" (Matt. 10:16).

"I have more understanding than all my teachers: for thy testimonies are my meditation" (Ps. 119:99). Why do the Scriptures

Not memorization, not rapid paced study, but meditation, the thoughtful contemplation of the knowledge at hand.

declare that students can have more understanding than all their teachers? David answers, "for thy testimonies are my *meditation*." Not memorization, not rapid paced study, but meditation, the thoughtful contemplation of the knowledge at hand. As has been for ages in the past, the education of students today is mainly based off of the memory. Students must memorize mass quantities of information to past a test, often with very limited time to do it. So much effort is given to the memorization of mere information that most students do not have the time necessary to prove the knowledge first to see if it is true, nor to assimilate the knowledge acquired. With no time to familiarize and meditate upon the information received, it exits the mind just as quickly as it enters. The knowledge has not had time to take root in the mind of the student and is quickly blown away. This is not God's plan for education.

Anything short of this is keeping the mind from being exercised in the lines where it should be and is just as much mind control as is forcing church doctrines upon an individual without giving them time to prove them first, *because that is what this is*. There is no time to search things out for themselves, because they must quickly memorize a bunch of information. And if students resist this form of mind control, pleading only the words of the apostles, "We ought to obey God rather than men" (Acts 5:29) what happens to them? They are judged as obstinate rebels who must be corrected. And it is true that they are obstinate rebels, but what are they rebelling against, sin or righteousness?

One of the best illustrations of the dangers of rapid-paced study and memorization without sufficient time to search the Scriptures, to "prove all things," *and then* "hold fast to that which is good" (1 Thess. 5:21), is the illustration of the man and the ducks. The man made a good loaf of bread, but before he baked it, he kneaded marble-sized rocks into the dough. Once baked, he let it cool, and then breaking it apart, he fed the bread to the ducks. But because ducks do not chew their food, but rather swallow it whole, they all choked on the rocks and died.

So it is with those who quickly memorize lots of information without first testing it to see if it is true. The students have no time to chew their food, no time to see if there is anything wrong with what they are being fed. There is no time to prove the information, thus many accept false teachings to their own condemnation.

Having mentioned time, many teachers encourage their students to make sure they spend time with God in personal devotions and prayer, even if it means failing to turn an assignment in on time or failing a test. The teachers well know that the student's strength to overcome temptation will be found in his time spent with the Savior. But the question is: does the workload that the teachers give their students make it conducive for them to spend time with Jesus? Students are

Chapter 1 — "The love of the truth"

often placed in the way of temptation by the very teachers who are trying to deliver them from it. As the result of their workload, the students are tempted to skip their time with Christ so they can finish their homework assignment or study for a test. Oh how sad. Why make it harder for the poor students who are struggling for eternal life? And if the student does overcome the temptation and chooses to spend his time with his Maker that he might have divine strength to resist temptation, what then happens to the student's grade? Do you see how the system works? The system itself has no mind, no reasoning capacities, no sense of justice.

Time and circumstances can keep students so busy that they cannot get the proper rest and relief from the heavy workload they are under. The laws of the human body cannot be kept under such a burden. The mind is taxed too heavily, and once nature can take the abuse no longer, disease finally settles in upon the student. And how is this breaking of nature's laws viewed by the Creator? "If any man defile the temple of God, him shall God destroy; for the temple of God is holy, which temple ye are" (1 Cor. 3:17). Do you see how this mindless system is set up to cause utter destruction to come upon the students?

> *In most cases, degrees, school policies, and church doctrines have taken the preeminence over useful knowledge, God's principles, and scriptural testimony.*

Some courses of theology today, as in Christ's time, make little of the great things and magnify those things that have little value. In most cases, degrees, school policies, and church doctrines have taken the preeminence over useful knowledge, God's principles, and scriptural testimony. But a woe is pronounced upon these types of people and institutions by Jesus Himself, "Woe unto you, scribes and Pharisees, hypocrites! for ye pay tithe of mint and anise and cummin, and have omitted the weightier matters of the law, judgment, mercy, and faith: these ought ye to have done, and not to leave the other undone. Ye blind guides, which strain at a gnat, and swallow a camel" (Matt. 23:23, 24).

It is a sin to assume upon others that things of little value are to be prized above all, while those things that are priceless are valued so little. How many times has a college degree been spoken of as holding great worth while useful knowledge has not been given its rightful preeminence? Is it the will of God for it to be this way? How many times has school policy punished a student when he or she was but carrying out what the Holy Spirit had placed upon his or her heart to do? The same problems arise when church doctrines are placed above the Word of God. Shall established church doctrines be allowed to take away our ability to think and reason for ourselves? "No prophecy of the scripture is of any private interpretation" (2 Peter 1:20). Our only creed is to be the Scriptures.

Another problem with today's educational system is the reward and punishment system. This system encourages the students to foster wrong motives for right doing. Thus the students are trained like dogs. "Do right," they are told, "and you'll get a treat; do wrong and you'll be punished. Be a faithful student by accepting as truth everything we say and doing good on your homework and tests, and we'll help get you where you need to be in life. Do wrong and perform poorly and you'll be assigned detention, suspension, or expulsion. Then you'll get nowhere in life, and your existence will be a waste, and everyone will look down on you."

What kind of thing is this? And what if it does correct the student's behavior? What then? The student will have the same sad testimony

Chapter 1 — "The love of the truth"

as king Asa: "he did that which was right in the sight of the LORD, *but not with a perfect heart*" (2 Chron. 25:2). The student has been trained to respond to rewards and punishments but has not made it a habit to respond to the love of God. How sad! Remove the rewards and punishments from the students, and they have no motive for right doing. Sadly, with no false motives to keep the students in line and no good ones established in their characters, many return to their foolish ways. "As a dog returneth to his vomit, so a fool returneth to his folly" (Prov. 26:11).

> *The student has been trained to respond to rewards and punishments but has not made it a habit to respond to the love of God.*

When a certain scribe came to Jesus and said, "Master, I will follow thee whithersoever thou goest," Jesus responded, "The foxes have holes, and the birds of the air have nests; but the Son of man hath not where to lay his head" (Matt. 8:19, 20). Jesus offered the scribe no hope of earthly reward for following Him. Jesus does not desire us to follow Him because we might receive some temporal blessing. He desires us to seek Him so that He might set us free from the power and the guilt of sin. "Verily, verily, I say unto you, Ye seek me, not because ye saw the miracles, but because ye did eat of the loaves, and were filled. Labour not for the meat which perisheth, but for that meat which endureth unto everlasting life, which the Son of man shall give unto you" (John 6:26, 27).

Jesus said "lay not up for yourselves treasures upon earth, where moth and rust doth corrupt, and where thieves break through and steal: But lay up for yourselves treasures in heaven, where neither moth nor rust doth corrupt, and where thieves do not break through nor steal:

For where your treasure is, there will your heart be also" (Matt. 6:19-21).

"The discipline of a human being who has reached the years of intelligence should differ from the training of a dumb animal. The beast is taught only submission to its master. For the beast, the master is mind, judgment, and will. This method, sometimes employed in the training of children, makes them little more than automatons. Mind, will, conscience, are under the control of another. It is not God's purpose that any mind should be thus dominated. Those who weaken or destroy individuality assume a responsibility that can result only in evil. While under authority, the children may appear like well-drilled soldiers; but when the control ceases, the character will be found to lack strength and steadfastness. Having never learned to govern himself, the youth recognizes no restraint except the requirement of parents or teacher. This removed, he knows not how to use his liberty, and often gives himself up to indulgence that proves his ruin" (Ellen G. White, *Education*, p. 288).

This is not to say that no punishment shall ever be given and that all order and discipline must be done away with, but punishment should by all means be avoided. However, if it cannot be avoided, it should be carried out because the individual *will not* submit to divine authority. It should never be enforced in an effort to submit his will and compel his compliance, for this is a false method of correction that often leads the individual to rebel even more rather than reform. In correcting others, we must remember that we ourselves are not perfect and are often found at variance with the law of God. In giving correction, that grandest of all principles must be obeyed, "All things whatsoever ye would that men should do to you, do ye even so to them" (Matt. 7:12).

The most common defense given in favor of the system of mind control is that there is more good in it than bad. It is true that once

Chapter 1 — "The love of the truth"

students complete a degree they will have been exposed to lots of information that they may never have come across on their own. This is a good thing. Furthermore, they will have a degree that will make it easier for them to get a good paying job. This is also a good thing. However, the weighty amount of good to be had is not worth the price of building a foundation on the sand.

If we were to understand that there is more good than bad in the system of mind control, then we must also understand that rat poisoning is also more good than bad. Take for instance rat poisoning—99.99 percent of rat poisoning is good food, only .01 percent of it is actually dangerous. With 99.99 percent of rat poisoning being good food, only .01 percent of it is actually dangerous.

> *Take for instance rat poisoning—99.99 percent of rat poisoning is good food, only .01 percent of it is actually dangerous.*

Take the rat poisoning, and you will suffer the sure results. Let the false system of education control your mind, and you will not be able to withstand the storm. "Be not deceived; God is not mocked: for whatsoever a man soweth, that shall he also reap" (Gal. 6:7). "What is a man profited, if he shall gain the whole world, *and lose his own soul?* or what shall a man give in exchange for his soul?" (Matt. 16:26).

It may be true that some people may need to use the false system in order to be able to witness to those who would otherwise never be reached by the gospel, but there is no one who can afford to be used by the false educational system. If need be, *we must use it*, but it must never be allowed to *use us*.

In today's society we face a system that tells us what we must believe, focuses on vain study and memorization, encourages the belittlement of importance and magnification of nothing, and subscribes to a reward and punishment system. These are the manipulative, mind-controlling principles of the machine. It is nothing but a lie. It promises education and success, but there is no true education and success outside of building upon the solid Rock and the Word of God. The promised success and education are lies, they do not exist, *except in the minds of those who accept and believe them.*

"Whoso shall offend one of these little ones which believe in me, it were better for him that a millstone were hanged about his neck, and that he were drowned in the depth of the sea" (Matt. 18:6). For the false teachers who have stolen away the ability of others to think and reason for themselves and thus caused their fall, the blood of their listeners will be upon them: "Woe unto you, lawyers! for ye have taken away the key of knowledge: ye entered not in yourselves, and them that were entering in ye hindered" (Luke 11:52).

"I say unto you, All manner of sin and blasphemy shall be forgiven unto men: but the blasphemy against the Holy Ghost shall not be forgiven unto men. And whosoever speaketh a word against the Son of man, it shall be forgiven him: but whosoever speaketh against the Holy Ghost, it shall not be forgiven him, neither in this world, neither in the world to come" (Matt. 12:31, 32).

But what exactly is the unpardonable sin against the Holy Ghost? "And the scribes which came down from Jerusalem said, He hath Beelzebub, and by the prince of the devils casteth he out devils. And he called them unto him, and said unto them in parables, How can Satan cast out Satan? And if a kingdom be divided against itself, that kingdom cannot stand. And if a house be divided against itself, that house cannot stand. And if Satan rise up against himself, and be divided, he cannot stand, but hath an end. No man can enter into a strong man's house, and spoil his goods, except he will first bind the strong man;

Chapter 1 — "The love of the truth"

and then he will spoil his house. Verily I say unto you, All sins shall be forgiven unto the sons of men, and blasphemies wherewith soever they shall blaspheme: But he that shall blaspheme against the Holy Ghost hath never forgiveness, but is in danger of eternal damnation. *Because they said, He hath an unclean spirit"* (Mark 3:22-30).

Why did Jesus say that those who sin against the Holy Ghost can never have forgiveness and are in danger of eternal damnation? *"Because they said, He hath an unclean spirit."* The Jew's had attributed to Satan the workings of the Holy Spirit wrought through Christ. *This is the unpardonable sin.* It is not that God shall not, or will not, forgive those who commit this sin, but He *cannot*. When God works upon their hearts to lead them to repentance and they insist upon believing that the workings of the Holy Spirit upon them is just the harassing voice of Satan, God cannot forgive them because *they will not accept the forgiveness*. They have chosen to believe that the repentance they are being called to is really just from Satan, and they *will not* accept it. God cannot help them, for all the help that He would so freely give, they would only attribute to the workings of satanic agencies and utterly reject it.

Now, what would be the danger in having stolen away from you the ability to reason, to think for yourself, and insist that what others have taught you is correct? The danger would be that when the Holy Spirit comes to convict you of truth you may very likely attribute the voice to Satan seeking to harass you, and therefore, you reject the Holy Spirit's guidance. Many poor souls cannot think for themselves because others are thinking for them! They have never learned how to think, and therefore, it is so difficult for their minds to be open to the Holy Spirit's influence. And oh how sad the final results of this may be! Again, "Whoso shall offend one of these little ones which believe in me, it were better for him that a millstone were hanged about his neck, and that he were drowned in the depth of the sea" (Matt. 18:6).

"To the law and to the testimony: if they speak not according to this word, it is because there is no light in them" (Isa. 8:20). Those whose teachings cannot stand up to the test of the law of God and the testimony of the Scriptures are teaching nothing more than fables. They teach well concerning those things that aren't real and that don't exist. They are liars, and however sincerely and honestly deceived they may be, their teachings are erroneous.

"Whom shall he teach knowledge? and whom shall he make to understand doctrine? them that are weaned from the milk, and drawn from the breasts. For precept must be upon precept, precept upon precept; line upon line, line upon line; here a little, and there a little" (Isa. 28:9, 10). Those who set themselves to the task of understanding what the Word of God says must follow the instruction given in the Bible on how to come to an understanding of it. Principle must be added to and compared with principle. One line of Scripture is to be read in the context of the line that precedes it and which it precedes, and we are to bring these principles and teachings from one part of the Bible a little, and from another part of the Bible a little. Thus bringing all of them together, they compose the puzzle pieces of the Master Artist's portrait, and with His aid in putting the pieces in their proper place, we will uncover the most beautiful of all artwork, the great breathtaking plan made for the redemption of the fallen race.

Everyone has the choice whether he will love the truth or love lies, and this may be done even when those deciding cannot yet point out the truth from error. In the day of final judgment, man will be condemned for loving lies over the truth. He will be condemned for believing in things that did not exist and not believing in the things that did. Make the choice to hate lies and love truth, to depend solely and only upon God to teach you what is truth. Take no man's say-so.

Chapter 1 — "The love of the truth"

Do not read the rest of this book, accepting whatever the author says as the pure truth of heaven. How will you know that what he is teaching is truth unless you first bring it to the test of the Scriptures and know for yourself that it is truth? And even if it is truth, you cannot accept it at the author's word without imperiling your soul. You must know it for yourself. You must build upon the Rock, the Word of God. Be a faithful Berean, as "these were more noble than those in Thessalonica, in that they received the word with all readiness of mind, *and searched the scriptures daily, whether those things were so*" (Acts 17:11).

Chapter 2

"He spake, and it was done"

Psalms 33:9

Are you ready?

"In the beginning God created the heaven and the earth. And the earth was without form, and void; and darkness was upon the face of the deep. And the Spirit of God moved upon the face of the waters. And *God said*, Let there be light: *and there was light.* . . . And *God said*, Let there be a firmament in the midst of the waters, and let it divide the waters from the waters . . . *and it was so.* . . . And *God said*, Let the waters under the heaven be gathered together unto one place, and let the dry land appear: *and it was so.* . . . And *God said*, Let the earth bring forth grass, the herb yielding seed, and the fruit tree yielding fruit after his kind, whose seed is in itself, upon the earth: *and it was so.* . . . And *God said*, Let there be lights in the firmament of the heaven to divide the day from the night; and let them be for signs, and for seasons, and for days, and years: And let them be for lights in the firmament of the heaven to give light upon the earth: *and it was so*" (Gen. 1:1-15). "And *God said*, Let the earth bring forth the living creature after his kind, cattle, and creeping thing, and beast of the earth after his kind: *and it was so*" (verse 24).

In the creation of the world, we see that there is creative power in the word of God to do what it says. "Let there be light," God said, "and

Chapter 2 — "He spake, and it was done"

there was light." The psalmist explains how things were created. "*By the word of the LORD were the heavens made; and all the host of them by the breath of his mouth. He gathereth the waters of the sea together as an heap: he layeth up the depth in storehouses. Let all the earth fear the LORD: let all the inhabitants of the world stand in awe of him. For he spake, and it was done; he commanded, and it stood fast*" (Ps. 33:6-9).

"Praise ye the LORD. Praise ye the LORD from the heavens: praise him in the heights. Praise ye him, all his angels: praise ye him, all his hosts. Praise ye him, sun and moon: praise him, all ye stars of light. Praise him, ye heavens of heavens, and ye waters that be above the heavens. Let them praise the name of the LORD: *for he commanded, and they were created*" (Ps. 148:1-5).

> *In the creation of the world, we see that there is creative power in the word of God to do what it says. "Let there be light," God said, "and there was light."*

It is important to notice from these scriptures that God's word itself is sufficient enough to do the thing that it says. If a man says that in six months there will be a completed house on a certain piece of property, than in order for that man's word to hold true he must either get others to build the house for him, or he must physically involve himself in constructing that house. He himself must lay the foundation; he himself must hit the nails with the hammer, etc. And he must also have that house completed by the end of those six months. But it is not this way with God's word.

The word of God itself has the power to create the thing it says without God having to be physically involved. "For as the rain cometh down, and the snow from heaven, and returneth not thither, but watereth the earth, and maketh it bring forth and bud, that it may give seed to the sower, and bread to the eater: *So shall my word be that goeth forth out of my mouth: it shall not return unto me void, but it shall accomplish that which I please, and it shall prosper in the thing whereto I sent it*" (Isa. 55:10, 11). What is the actual thing that accomplishes that which God pleases? The *word* that goes forth out of His mouth, *it* shall accomplish His pleasure.

This is how God creates things and accomplishes His pleasure—He speaks and it is. The creative power that lies within the word of God is the only thing necessary to accomplish the thing that it says. If God speaks the word, and speaks the word *only*, without doing a single other thing, that thing which He spoke is done.

The Scriptures teach that God "cannot lie," and in even stronger language, the Bible says that it is "impossible for God to lie" (Titus 1:2; Heb. 6:18). The reason that God cannot possibly lie is because of the creative power that is within His spoken word. Should God say that there is a fire-breathing dragon behind you, you should grab your shield, draw your sword, and turn square about, because the words that God spoke will themselves create that dragon. Paul teaches that God "calleth those things which be not as though they were" (Rom. 4:17). Now, if a man talks about something that isn't as though it was, he is a liar. But when God talks about something that isn't as though it was, He is not a liar because if God says that something is the creative power of His spoken word creates it. His word alone calls it into existence.

> *The reason that God cannot possibly lie is because of the creative power that is within His spoken word.*

This is one of the greatest evidences that God's creation is instant.

Chapter 2 — "He spake, and it was done"

If God's creation wasn't instant, then it would be possible for God to lie. Looking at the example again, if God said that there is a fire-breathing dragon behind you, if it took even two seconds before that fire-breathing dragon appeared, then God would be a liar for those two seconds. Therefore, since it is impossible for God to lie, God's creation must be instant.

What greater evidence can be given that the words of God are true than the understanding of why it is perfectly impossible for God to lie? It is true that there has been and still is so much perverting of the Scriptures, rewritings of the Bible, that it seems that there is no hope that the words of God remain pure and accurate, but the Lord has made provision so that His Holy Word will not be destroyed. The creative word of God declares, "The words of the LORD are pure words: as silver tried in a furnace of earth, purified seven times. Thou shalt keep them, O LORD, thou shalt preserve them from this generation for ever" (Ps. 12:6, 7).

These words of Scripture, which "came not in old time by the will of man" (2 Peter 1:21) but were "given by inspiration of God" (2 Tim. 3:16), declare that while the words of the Lord may be tested and tried, they will remain pure and will be preserved forever. Since the word of God itself has power to accomplish the thing it says, we have the strongest reason to believe that God's Word will remain pure and uncorrupted. Why? Because the word of God *said* that it will. No matter how much the forces of apostasy may seek to pervert and destroy the Word of God, no matter how much rubbish may be dumped upon the Scriptures in effort to bury it beneath a mass of lies, the Word of God will still remain, like a diamond among the gravel, pure and undefiled. "The grass withereth, the flower fadeth: but the word of our God shall stand for ever" (Isa. 40:8). And, says the Lord, "Heaven and earth shall pass away, but my words shall not pass away" (Matt.

24:35). If the Scriptures are God's message to man, do you think He would let wicked, finite men destroy that message?

The things that the word of God creates, it also sustains. "God, who at sundry times and in divers manners spake in time past unto the fathers by the prophets, Hath in these last days spoken unto us by his Son, whom he hath appointed heir of all things, by whom also he made the worlds; Who being the brightness of his glory, and the express image of his person, *and upholding all things by the word of his power*, when he had by himself purged our sins, sat down on the right hand of the Majesty on high" (Heb. 1:1-3).

The created world exists only because the word of God created it and has caused it to continue to exist throughout the ages. "There shall come in the last days scoffers, walking after their own lusts, And saying, Where is the promise of his coming? for since the fathers fell asleep, all things continue as they were from the beginning of the creation. For this they willingly are ignorant of, that by the word of God the heavens were of old, and the earth standing out of the water and in the water: Whereby the world that then was, being overflowed with water, perished: But the heavens and the earth, which are now, *by the same word are kept in store*, reserved unto fire against the day of judgment and perdition of ungodly men" (2 Peter 3:3-7).

It is not that God first creates something by one word and then speaks another word to sustain that creation, God's creation is "by *the same word*" kept in store. The word of God that creates the thing it says is the same word that also sustains it.

"Praise ye the LORD. Praise ye the LORD from the heavens: praise him in the heights. Praise ye him, all his angels: praise ye him, all his hosts. Praise ye him, sun and moon: praise him, all ye stars of light. Praise him, ye heavens of heavens, and ye waters that be above the heavens. Let them praise the name of the LORD: *for he commanded, and they were created. He hath also stablished them for ever and ever: he hath made a decree which shall not pass*" (Ps. 148:1-6).

Chapter 3

"Speak the word only"

Matthew 8:8

Are you ready?

"When he [Jesus] was come down from the mountain, great multitudes followed him. And, behold, there came a leper and worshipped him, saying, Lord, if thou wilt, thou canst make me clean. And Jesus put forth his hand, and touched him, saying, I will; *be thou clean*. And *immediately* his leprosy was cleansed" (Matt. 8:1-3).

The word of God in itself has power to do the thing it says. Jesus spoke the word to the leper saying, "Be thou clean." Nothing else was necessary for that word to accomplish the thing it said. The word alone was sufficient enough to cleanse the man of his leprosy. And not only did the word cleanse the leper of his leprosy, but it cleansed him *immediately*. There was no gradual or even rapid change from leprosy to life. No, it was an instant change. "*As soon* as He had spoken, *immediately* the leprosy departed from him, and he was cleansed" (Mark 1:42).

"And when Jesus was entered into Capernaum, there came unto him a centurion, beseeching him, And saying, Lord, my servant lieth at home sick of the palsy, grievously tormented. And Jesus saith unto him, I will come and heal him. The centurion answered and said, Lord, I am not worthy that thou shouldest come under my roof: but speak

Chapter 3 — "Speak the word only"

the word only, and my servant shall be healed. For I am a man under authority, having soldiers under me: and I say to this man, Go, and he goeth; and to another, Come, and he cometh; and to my servant, Do this, and he doeth it. When Jesus heard it, he marvelled, and said to them that followed, Verily I say unto you, I have not found so great faith, no, not in Israel" (Matt. 8:5-10).

> *The word of God in itself has power to do the thing it says… The word alone was sufficient enough to cleanse the man of his leprosy.*

"Speak the word *only*." These words are full of meaning! Upon hearing his request, Jesus agrees to come and heal the centurion's servant. But the respected centurion, feeling unworthy that Jesus should come to his home, replies, "*Speak the word only, and my servant shall be healed.*" The centurion acknowledged that the word of Christ *alone* was sufficient enough *of itself* to do the thing that it said. He knew that it wasn't necessary for Christ to be physically involved in healing his servant. No, the word *only* was sufficient. Now, when Jesus heard this, "he marvelled, and said to them that followed, Verily I say unto you, I have not found so *great faith*, no, not in Israel."

Jesus said that this centurion had "great faith." But what did this centurion do? Why does Jesus declare him as being a possessor of great faith? All that the centurion did was *acknowledge* the power of the word of Christ to do the thing it said, *know* that it would do what it said, and *depend* upon that word *alone* to do it. And it was this that Christ declared as "great faith."

"And again he [Jesus] entered into Capernaum after some days; and it was noised that he was in the house. And straightway many were gathered together, insomuch that there was no room to receive them, no, not so much as about the door: and he preached the word unto them. And they come unto him, bringing one sick of the palsy, which was borne of four. And when they could not come nigh unto him for the press, they uncovered the roof where he was: and when they had broken it up, they let down the bed wherein the sick of the palsy lay. When Jesus saw their faith, he said unto the sick of the palsy, Son, thy sins be forgiven thee.

"But there were certain of the scribes sitting there, and reasoning in their hearts, Why doth this man thus speak blasphemies? who can forgive sins but God only? And immediately when Jesus perceived in his spirit that they so reasoned within themselves, he said unto them, Why reason ye these things in your hearts? Whether is it easier to say to the sick of the palsy, Thy sins be forgiven thee; or to say, Arise, and take up thy bed, and walk? But that ye may know that the Son of man hath power on earth to forgive sins, (he saith to the sick of the palsy,) I say unto thee, Arise, and take up thy bed, and go thy way into thine house. And immediately he arose, took up the bed, and went forth before them all; insomuch that they were all amazed, and glorified God, saying, We never saw it on this fashion" (Mark 2:1-12).

"Son, thy sins be forgiven thee." The word of Christ is sufficient enough to do the thing that it says; the word of God cannot lie. The instant that Jesus spoke these words to the palsied sinner, no matter how sinful his life may have been, no matter how much a child of the devil he once was, this man was forgiven. He was instantly re-created as a "son" of God. Why? It is because Jesus called him His son. The word of Christ alone was sufficient enough of make him a child of heaven. The word of Christ alone applied God's forgiveness to his soul and set him free from the guilt of his sins.

"Arise, and take up thy bed, and go thy way." This palsied man was on a bed because he could not move as a result of his palsy. But

Chapter 3 — "Speak the word only"

the word of Christ was sufficient enough of itself to cause the man to rise, take up his bed, and walk. The word "arise" was the word of healing, and that word alone was enough to heal the man of his palsy. And what was the result of the word of Christ? "*Immediately* he arose, took up the bed, and went forth."

It was then that Christ might have said to that man as He said to His disciples, "Now ye are clean *through the word which I have spoken unto you*" (John 15:3). This man was not merely healed of his palsy but cleansed from his sins. And how was this made possible? It was through the word that Christ had spoken. The blood that He was yet to shed that it might wash this sinner clean from his iniquities at that moment was applied to his soul through the words of the Savior.

"And when Jesus departed thence, two blind men followed him, crying, and saying, Thou son of David, have mercy on us. And when he was come into the house, the blind men came to him: and Jesus saith unto them, Believe ye that I am able to do this? They said unto him, Yea, Lord. Then touched he their eyes, saying, According to your faith be it unto you. And their eyes were opened" (Matt. 9:27-30).

"Believe ye that I am able to do this?" What a searching question! Oh what eternal results rest upon our answer! Paul speaks of Christ as the One "that is able to keep you from falling, and to present you faultless before the presence of his glory" (Jude 1:24), and the Savior's question to you is, "Believe ye that I am able to do this?" Let the Lord Himself help you answer this question: "Behold," He says, "I am the LORD, the God of all flesh: *is there any thing too hard for me?*" (Jer. 32:27). Paul was confident that Christ was *able* to keep him from falling, but he goes even further to say that we should be "confident of this very thing, that he which hath begun a good work in you *will perform it* until the day of Jesus Christ" (Phil. 1:6). Jesus asks us only this one thing, "Believe ye that I am able to do this?" And if you believe that He is able, then "according to your faith *be it unto you.*"

"According to your faith be it unto you." Faith, according to Jesus' definition, is dependence upon the word of God *alone* to do what it says. This is simply to say that the instant you exercise saving faith by depending upon the word of Christ alone to do what it says, *it is unto you*—you instantly have the gift that the word promised. And what was the result of the blind men's dependence on Christ's words? "Their eyes were opened." But suppose that the men had not depended upon the word of Christ alone to do what it said. What would have happened then? It is simple, according to their faith it would have been unto them. They would have remained blind.

Faith has always been and always will be the essential part in receiving God's promised blessing. "All things, whatsoever ye shall ask in prayer, *believing,* ye shall receive" (Matt. 21:22). Furthermore, "this is the confidence that we have in him, that, if we ask any thing according to his will, he heareth us" (1 John 5:14). Because of the creative characteristic of the word of God, it is impossible for God to lie. If Christ promises to forgive our sins and we do not believe that He will, we are calling Him a liar. "He that believeth not God hath made him a liar; because he believeth not the record that God gave" (1 John 5:10). When we declare God a liar through our unbelief, we ourselves are lying, because it is impossible for God to lie. Whatever He says must be true, because if it wasn't true before He said it, it became true by the time He was done saying it. God cannot bless the one who calls Him a liar, for the condition of receiving the promised blessing is that he believes that God's promised word is true. Not that it will be true, but that it *is* true.

"And, behold, a man of the company cried out, saying, Master, I beseech thee, look upon my son: for he is mine only child. And, lo, a

Chapter 3 — "Speak the word only"

spirit taketh him" (Luke 9:38, 39).

"And wheresoever he taketh him, he teareth him: and he foameth, and gnasheth with his teeth, and pineth away: and I spake to thy disciples that they should cast him out; and they could not. He answereth him, and saith, O faithless generation, how long shall I be with you? how long shall I suffer you? bring him unto me. And they brought him unto him: and when he saw him, straightway the spirit tare him; and he fell on the ground, and wallowed foaming. And he asked his father, How long is it ago since this came unto him? And he said, Of a child. And ofttimes it hath cast him into the fire, and into the waters, to destroy him: but if thou canst do any thing, have compassion on us, and help us.

"Jesus said unto him, If thou canst believe, all things are possible to him that believeth. And straightway the father of the child cried out, and said with tears, Lord, I believe; help thou mine unbelief. When Jesus saw that the people came running together, he rebuked the foul spirit, saying unto him, Thou dumb and deaf spirit, I charge thee, come out of him, and enter no more into him. And the spirit cried, and rent him sore, and came out of him: and he was as one dead; insomuch that many said, He is dead. But Jesus took him by the hand, and lifted him up; and he arose" (Mark 9:18-27).

"If thou canst do any thing, have compassion on us." If? Why if? Is not Christ able to do the thing He says? Is not His word sufficient enough to restore the father's child? Indeed it is, but the father questioned the power of Christ. Jesus could not bless the request of unbelief, and instead He responded, "If thou canst believe, all things are possible to him that believeth." When Christ spoke these words, it was then that the father realized that the only hope of his child being healed was dependent upon his faith in Christ. He knew that his unbelief would cost the life of his child, or worse. Not able to endure it any longer "straightway the father of the child cried out, and said with tears, Lord, I believe; help thou mine unbelief" (Mark 9:24).

"Lord, I believe; help thou mine unbelief." These words are overflowing with faith. This man, in his utter helplessness, had to depend upon Christ *alone* for the healing of his son. Saving faith *is* dependence upon Christ. Saving faith is dependence upon the Word to do what it says. The son of the father was healed, and this testifies to the faith that the father exercised. "Lord, I believe; help thou mine unbelief." In these words is expressed the father's realization of his utter inability. Realizing that his son's only hope was in Jesus, the father threw his whole soul into the hands of Christ and depended solely upon Him to heal his son. He had no other choice. He could either depend solely on Jesus or lose his son.

This is a case that reveals to a deeper level a vital point of saving faith. Saving faith in Christ is dependence upon the word *alone*, that His word will do what it says. The father realized that he could do nothing to save his son from the demon that possessed him. He was perfectly powerless to affect this even to the least degree. He could not depend upon anything he could or would do, for he could literally do *nothing*. He had to depend upon Christ *alone, solely, and only*. And it was upon doing this that Christ brought healing to his son.

How many times in life do we come to a position of need and, feeling faithless, stay away from Jesus because we know that He cannot help us while we are unbelieving. But feelings have nothing to do with faith. Faith is not *feeling* that Christ will do what He said. Faith is *dependence* upon Christ that He will do what He said. Since you believe that it is impossible for God to lie, then you know that the Word of God is true. This is all the faith that is needed. It requires no great effort. It requires no great sacrifice. It is just a simple acknowledgment that Christ's word is true. And how hard is that?

Chapter 3 — "Speak the word only"

How hard is it to depend upon someone else to do everything for you?

"And a certain man was there, which had an infirmity thirty and eight years. When Jesus saw him lie, and knew that he had been now a long time in that case, he saith unto him, Wilt thou be made whole? The impotent man answered him, Sir, I have no man, when the water is troubled, to put me into the pool: but while I am coming, another steppeth down before me. Jesus saith unto him, Rise, take up thy bed, and walk. And immediately the man was made whole, and took up his bed, and walked" (John 5:5-9).

Again, this is a case of dire need, and again the lovely Jesus speaks the word of healing to the believing one, and once again, "immediately" a change is wrought. Oh compassionate Savior! The harlot's best friend! There He is, the King of the heavenly universe, not too high to stoop and heal the sick, not too holy to wash the vile sinner's feet.

With what tenderness and pity does He look upon those whom He has created in His own image who have been deceived by Satan and wounded by sin

With what tenderness and pity does He look upon those whom He has created in His own image who have been deceived by Satan and wounded by sin. His desire is only to restore them that they might enjoy His presence and feel the warmth of His love. But oh how many stay away from Him because they don't understand Him who is "altogether lovely"? (Song of Sol. 5:16).

"And the scribes and Pharisees brought unto him a woman taken in adultery; and when they had set her in the midst, They say unto him, Master, this woman was taken in adultery, in the very act. Now Moses in the law commanded us, that such should be stoned: but what sayest thou? This they said, tempting him, that they might have to accuse him. But Jesus stooped down, and with his finger wrote on the ground, as though he heard them not. So when they continued asking him, he lifted up himself, and said unto them, He that is without sin among you, let him first cast a stone at her. And again he stooped down, and wrote on the ground. And they which heard it, being convicted by their own conscience, went out one by one, beginning at the eldest, even unto the last: and Jesus was left alone, and the woman standing in the midst. When Jesus had lifted up himself, and saw none but the woman, he said unto her, Woman, where are those thine accusers? hath no man condemned thee? She said, No man, Lord. And Jesus said unto her, Neither do I condemn thee: go, and sin no more" (John 8:3-11).

"Neither do I condemn thee." How many "Christians" would stick up their nose and look down upon this poor woman as nothing but a dirty harlot deserving of punishment? Or, to make it seem more holy, how many would shed a tear for her lost condition and look upon her as hopeless? Hopeless!? "He that is without sin among you, let him first cast a stone at her." Jesus understood this woman. While He would not justify her *sin*, He would justify *her*. As sinners, humans seek to judge and condemn to death, but the lovely Jesus seeks only to justify and restore.

"Go, and sin no more." While seeming to be just instruction, within these words laid the power to keep the woman from sinning. The words of Christ are able of themselves to do the thing they said. The only requirement for this woman to receive the promised victory

Chapter 3 — "Speak the word only"

over all sin was that she depend upon that word *only* to keep her from sinning.

Let's now look at a story in Mark 10:46-52: "And they came to Jericho: and as he went out of Jericho with his disciples and a great number of people, blind Bartimaeus, the son of Timaeus, sat by the highway side begging. And when he heard that it was Jesus of Nazareth, he began to cry out, and say, Jesus, thou son of David, have mercy on me. And many charged him that he should hold his peace: but he cried the more a great deal, Thou son of David, have mercy on me. And Jesus stood still, and commanded him to be called. And they call the blind man, saying unto him, Be of good comfort, rise; he calleth thee. And he, casting away his garment, rose, and came to Jesus. And Jesus answered and said unto him, What wilt thou that I should do unto thee? The blind man said unto him, Lord, that I might receive my sight. And Jesus said unto him, Go thy way; thy faith hath made thee whole. And immediately he received his sight, and followed Jesus in the way."

"What wilt thou that I should do unto thee?" This question is not just to Bartimaeus but to all who are in need. And what is it, dear soul, that you would like Him to do for you? Should you desire of Him that He forgive your sins, set you free from the weighty guilt of your past life, and enable you to live happily with victory over those sins and habits that you yourself hate, His answer would unhesitatingly be, "According to your faith be it unto you." "Be thou clean." "Thy sins be forgiven thee." He asks of you no great thing. He asks of you no great sacrifice or heavy drudgery. He only asks that you depend upon

> *He only asks that you depend upon Him alone and believe that He will do what He said*

Salvation Isn't Free... It's Been Paid For!

Him alone and believe that He will do what He said—forgive your sins and keep you from sinning. And then know, dear soul, that even the moment you do this, *it is unto you*. Feelings mean nothing, emotions mean nothing, but the knowledge that you have truly been forgiven and set free from the power of sin, this in itself will mean everything to you and will be the channel that brings the sweet peace of heaven into your heart.

Chapter 4

"God spake all these words"

Exodus 20:1

Are you ready?

The law of God, expressed in the Ten Commandments given at Mount Sinai, was *spoken* straight from the mouth of God. "And God *spake* all these words, saying, I am the LORD thy God, which have brought thee out of the land of Egypt, out of the house of bondage. Thou shalt have no other gods before me" (Ex. 20:1-3). What this means is that just like all of the other words that God speaks, the law of God itself has creative power to do the thing that it says. And not only does it have the power to do the thing it says, but it is sufficient enough of itself to do the thing that it says without any physical involvement necessary to accomplish what it says.

Let us look at a familiar promise found in the book of Isaiah. "When thou passest through the waters, I will be with thee; and through the rivers, they shall not overflow thee: when thou walkest through the fire, *thou shalt not* be burned; neither shall the flame kindle upon thee" (Isa. 43:2). Notice the words "thou shalt not" in the text. When reading the Ten Commandments, so often the words "thou shalt not" are merely read as the introduction to

The law of God itself has creative power to do the thing that it says.

another command—read as if they were just about to introduce another restriction placed upon sinful man. But the book of Isaiah reveals that the words "thou shalt not" are the introduction to a promise.

How precious is the law of God to us! So often we find ourselves hating the very sins that we commit over and over again. We long for deliverance from these habits of wickedness that control us as if we were lifeless puppets with no mind or will. We strive to break free from these sins that are ruining our lives and the lives of the ones we love, but when temptation comes, we find that we are less than powerless to escape. The solution to our problem is found where we have least expected it. That very law which unmistakably points out our sins and shows us our guilt is the only thing that can set us free from the power of sin.

> *That very law which unmistakably points out our sins and shows us our guilt is the only thing that can set us free from the power of sin.*

The commandment "Thou shalt not commit adultery" is so often read with the connotation of, "You are not allowed to commit adultery." But this is *not* the connotation that God desires us to read His commandments with. That was not His original intention. The seventh commandment is to be literally read as the seventh promise, and it is to be understood with the following connotation of joy, "You will not commit adultery anymore." Isn't that wonderful!? In essence, God is saying, "You will no longer have to wallow around in guilt for continually committing this sin because I am promising you that you will no longer do it. Not only have I forgiven your past sins, but I am assuring you that you will not commit this sin anymore as long as you believe that you won't."

By depending upon the commandment alone, that it will do what

Chapter 4 — "God spake all these words"

it says, we are set free from that power which would drive us deeper and deeper into sin. As long as we depend upon the commandment alone to do what it says, we are safe. But should we depend upon anything other than this to keep us from sinning, we are at the mercy of the wicked one. Our only safety is in Christ, the Word of God. Depending upon Him *alone*, we have victory. Depending upon Him *and* what we are able to do, we will fail.

"Thy word have I hid in mine heart, that I might not sin against thee" (Ps. 119:11). When the Word/law of God is in the heart, then we are safe from sin. But how can we put the Word in our heart? It is very simple; we cannot put the word in our heart. "This is the covenant that I will make with them after those days, saith the Lord, *I will* put my laws into their hearts, and in their minds will I write them" (Heb. 10:16). God is the One who will put His law into our hearts. "I will," He said. That means Him, not you. And how does God accomplish His pleasure in putting His law in our hearts? "My word," He says, "*it* shall accomplish that which I please" (Isa. 55:11).

The Word of God itself is the thing that puts itself within our hearts. But God does not force His law upon us; He gives us the choice whether or not we will choose to live by the principles of love. So then, since God uses no force, what is it that we must do in order for the Word of God to put itself within us?

The promise of God is, "I will put my laws into their hearts" (Heb. 10:16). Since this is a promise, we are to receive its fulfillment to us in the same way that we receive all the promises of God, *by faith*. We are to receive the fulfillment of this promise by *depending* upon that promise of God alone to put itself within our hearts and knowing that since we do this *it is in our hearts*.

When we believe the above promise and accept the commandments of God into our hearts by faith, depending upon them *alone* to do what they say, at that *instant* the law of God is written in our heart and we can say with the psalmist, "I *delight* to do thy will, O my God: yea, *thy law is within my heart*" (Ps. 40:8). When God's law is in the heart, we actually enjoy doing God's will. It is our highest pleasure. *We really do not want to commit sin,* because we would rather delight ourselves in doing the will of God.

Since every command of God is a creative promise, which is able of itself to keep you from sinning, without any physical involvement from you, and it is God's will for you to keep His law, you can therefore safely conclude that if you will depend upon the commandment of God alone to keep you from sinning, you may be assured with unmistakable evidence that "according to your faith be *it* unto you" (Matt. 9:29).

> *When God's law is in the heart, we actually enjoy doing God's will.*

"To him that knoweth to do good, and doeth it not, to him it is sin" (James 4:17). "Sin is the transgression of the law" (1 John 3:4). If we know that we should do that which is good and we do not do it, then we are breaking the law of God. "The wages of sin" has been, and forever will be, "death" (Rom. 6:23). But when good works need to be done, they are to be done by Christ. Back in the days of creation, "He commanded, and they were created" (Ps. 148:5). So it is to be in our lives today. He commands of us good works, and the good works are created. As for the actual doing of the good works, *it is enough* that God commanded them to be. "For God, who commanded the light to shine out of darkness, hath shined in our hearts, to give the light of the knowledge of the glory of God in the face of Jesus Christ" (2 Cor. 4:6).

Chapter 5

"I the LORD have created it"

Isaiah 45:8

Are you ready?

"Behold, the days come, saith the LORD, that I will make a new covenant with the house of Israel, and with the house of Judah: Not according to the covenant that I made with their fathers in the day that I took them by the hand to bring them out of the land of Egypt; which my covenant they brake, although I was an husband unto them, saith the LORD: But this shall be the covenant that I will make with the house of Israel; After those days, saith the LORD, I will put my law in their inward parts, and write it in their hearts; and will be their God, and they shall be my people" (Jer. 31:31-33).

The promise that God will write His law in our hearts is the new covenant *promise*. The way for man to receive the fulfillment of this promise is the same way that we receive the fulfillment of all promises, *by faith*. And because of the creative nature of the word, the instant that we believe the promise, we *have* the law written on our heart. Each commandment itself is a promise, and the way for those promises to be written on our hearts is for us to believe them.

Notice that the new covenant promise does not say that the law of God is changed or done away with, but that the very same law is *perpetuated*, only its now written on the heart of man instead of upon tables of stone. God has never needed to change His law, for "the law of the LORD is perfect, converting the soul" (Ps. 19:7). And Jesus said, "Till heaven and earth pass, one jot or one tittle shall in no wise pass from the law, till all be fulfilled" (Matt. 5:18). Jesus says that as long as heaven and earth have not yet passed away the law of God will stand unchanged in the least. Heaven is still there, and earth is still here, and God's law therefore remains the same, to be perpetuated in the heart of man through the new covenant promise. "The wages of sin is death" (Rom. 6:23), and "the unrighteous shall not inherit the kingdom of God" (1 Cor. 6:9), but God has made "a way to escape" (1 Cor. 10:13) for us, that through faith alone, sins can be forgiven and sin can be overcome. "The gift of God is eternal life through Jesus Christ our Lord" (Rom. 6:23).

The new covenant promise is also found in the book of Ezekiel. "Then will I sprinkle clean water upon you, and ye shall be clean: from all your filthiness, and from all your idols, will I cleanse you. A new heart also will I give you, and a new spirit will I put within you: and I will take away the stony heart out of your flesh, and I will give you an heart of flesh. And *I will put my spirit within you*, and cause you to walk in my statutes, and ye shall keep my judgments, and do them" (Eze. 36:25-27).

Notice that the new covenant promise involves God putting His Spirit in us. The apostle Paul, when quoting the new covenant promise says, "And what agreement hath the temple of God with idols? for ye are the temple of the living God; as God hath said, *I will dwell in them*, and walk in them; and I will be their God, and they shall be my people" (2 Cor. 6:16). To have the new covenant promise fulfilled means to have God abiding in your heart, and since Jesus is God (John 1:1, 14), the new covenant promise is the promise "that Christ may dwell in your hearts *by faith*" (Eph. 3:17). But faith in what? Faith in

Chapter 5 — "I the LORD have created it"

the promise. It is through exercising faith in the new covenant promise that Christ dwells in our hearts.

"Whosoever is born of God doth not commit sin; for his seed remaineth in him: and he cannot sin, because he is born of God" (1 John 3:9). What is the seed in this verse? If you were to take it symbolically, "the seed is the word of God" (Luke 8:11) and Jesus is "the Word of God" (Rev. 19:13; see also John 1:1, 14). If you were to take it literally, a seed is a child. "And Adam knew his wife again; and she bare a son, and called his name Seth: For God, said she, hath appointed me *another seed* instead of Abel, whom Cain slew" (Gen. 4:25; see also Gal. 3:16). So a seed is a child, and Jesus Christ is "the Son of God" (Mark 1:1). Either way, God's seed in 1 John 3:9 is referring to Jesus. And what does the verse say is the result of Jesus dwelling in us? It does not say that we will not, or shall not sin, but it says that we *cannot*; it is impossible!

What is the reason that man cannot transgress the law when Christ is in his heart? Is it because man is in control of God's power? Or, is it because the creative power of God is in control of him? It is the latter.

That is not to say that if a man "believes" that Christ is in his heart and he knowingly breaks God's commandments that it is not sin. God has made it very clear what sin is: "Sin is the transgression of the law" (1 John 3:4). Who's law? "There is one lawgiver, who is able to save and to destroy" (James 4:12). "The LORD is our lawgiver" (Isa. 33:22). If man believes that since Christ is in his heart he can violate God's law without sinning, such a man is calling God a liar. God says, "Sin is the transgression of the law," while man says,

"Sin is not the transgression of the law, because I transgress the law without sinning." Whom do you believe? The righteous God who cannot lie, or sinful man? Let the apostle Paul help you answer this question. He says, "Let God be true, but every man a liar" (Rom. 3:4). Such a faith, one that leads men to transgress God's law, is not faith but presumption.

It needs to be made unmistakably clear here. Why is it that man cannot break the law when Christ is in his heart? First of all, what is it that said that when Christ is in the heart of man that that man cannot sin? The all-powerful creative word of God said it. Therefore *it has to be true*. So then, what is the reason that man cannot transgress the law when Christ is in his heart? Is it because man is in control of God's power? Or, is it because the creative power of God is in control of him? It is the latter. It is because the instant the soul accepts Christ into his heart he is now under the creative power of the word of God (1 John 3:9), and that word declares that sin shall not be manifested in his life.

Chapter 6

"Kept by the power of God"

1 Peter 1:5

Are you ready?

The rule of faith is "according to your faith be it unto you" (Matt. 9:29). This rule holds true both ways. If a man's dependence upon the Word of God *alone* to do what it says remains firm, then according to his dependence, *it is* unto him. But if man's dependence upon the Word of God *alone* to do what it says does not remain firm, if he doubts, then according to his dependence, so it is unto him, which is simply to say that it isn't unto him because he is not exercising true faith.

Satan knows that when man accepts Christ into his heart, by exercising faith in God's promise, the power of the creative word of God will keep that man from committing sin. Satan cannot change this. He is powerless against the almighty word of God. All the powers of earth and hell cannot force the believing child of God to commit sin because the word of God keeps him from sinning. It would be a waste of Satan's time to try to force man into sinning when God's word keeps him from it. Satan cannot change the creative promises of God, nor can he

> *Satan cannot change the creative promises of God, nor can he repel their power...*

repel their power, but if he can get man to doubt the promise of God, instantly the creative word will cease to be exercised in his behalf and Satan can then gain the victory over man and cause him to sin.

Satan has certain tactics he uses to influence man to doubt God's promises. These tactics that Satan uses *are the temptations* we meet. The temptations of the devil are solely calculated to get man to doubt the Word of God because this is *the only way* that he can overcome the human agent. If he fails to do this, the creative word of God will keep the believing soul from committing sin. As long as man continues to exercise faith in God by depending upon His Word *alone* to do what it says, to keep him from sinning, Satan will stand miserably defeated.

Satan tempts us both through thoughts and through feelings. But when Satan tempts us, he does not want it to appear like he is tempting us. If he did this, we would instantly flee to God so that He could overcome the temptation for us. So instead of coming out and saying, "This is Satan. I am tempting you and I want you to commit adultery," he inserts his temptation into our minds *like it is our own thought.* The temptation comes to our mind like this, "Wow! That person is sexy. I really want to go to bed with them." Through that insinuated thought, Satan then excites feelings in our body that causes us to crave sex. At this point in time, Satan may cunningly quote to us the words of Scripture saying, "As [a man] thinketh in his heart, so is he" (Prov. 23:7). He continues, "Out of the heart proceed evil thoughts, murders, adulteries, fornications, thefts, false witness, blasphemies: These are the things which defile a man" (Matt. 15:19, 20).

If in the moment of temptation we believe God's creative promises and accept them, we have a new and good heart from God. God's law written within our heart, and we therefore actually enjoy doing God's will by keeping His commandments. We really do not *want* sin. And not only that, but God has promised us that we shall not commit

Chapter 6 — "Kept by the power of God"

adultery. But Satan wants us to doubt these promises.

The reason that Satan is so successful in seducing us into sin is because *his temptations come to us in such a way as to assume upon us that we already want sin*, that we already desire it. He assumes upon us that sin therefore already exists in the heart, that the heart is already defiled, and that it therefore cannot be much more of a sin to follow through with the action. But it is all a lie! It is not true, and it does not exist. Temptation is not a sin; the sin is yielding to temptation.

It doesn't appear to us as a lie because that would destroy Satan's plan.

When Satan runs an evil thought through our mind and excites in us an evil feeling, both the evil thought and the evil feeling is nothing but a *lie*. But it doesn't appear to us as a lie because that would destroy Satan's plan. If man chooses to live by feelings, then as far as that man is concerned, temptation is the truth. And since he believes Satan's lie, he believes that Satan is true and inevitably must therefore doubt God's promise and declare God a liar. There is no hope for such an unbelieving one. Unbelief in the promises of the law, that they themselves will keep you from sinning, cut off the channel through which they are fulfilled to us. The only hope for such a man as this is for him to claim the promises of the law of God by faith, to acknowledge God as true, that God's Word is true, and to acknowledge this *in behalf of his own soul*. Then Satan will be instantly vanquished by the creative word of God.

Temptations come from Satan and from the evil of our own hearts. These are the only two sources of our temptations. Christ was "in the wilderness forty days, *tempted of Satan*" (Mark 1:13), and the apostle James says, "Every man is tempted, when he is drawn away *of his own lust*, and enticed" (James 1:14).

Now, if we believe the promise of God that we have a new heart, then that very creative promise of God fulfills itself to us by instantly creating in us a good heart. And since our heart is good, when we find ourselves tempted to do evil, we can know that the temptation to sin is just a masterful deception of Satan and that it is not coming from our own heart. But, in the moment of temptation, should we doubt the promise of God by believing Satan's lie, that we really want to do evil, then God's promise will cease to be fulfilled in us. Then the lie of Satan will become true because the word of God has been cut off by our unbelief, and the same word that created us anew in Christ can no longer uphold and sustain that good heart which it created. Our heart will become corrupt, and Satan can then wreck havoc upon us.

Temptation, as has been clearly shown, is resisted by faith *alone*. The promise of the Word is, "Resist the devil, and he will flee from you" (James 4:7). When we are tempted to sin, if we will just resist the temptation through faith in the Word, the devil will flee from us. And it is not just that he will flee, but that he is forced to flee. "Resist the devil, and he will flee from you." These words carry with them the creative power of God to do what they say. Meet the condition, and the promise will be fulfilled. It is then just a matter of time before the word of God forces Satan to flee.

Chapter 7

"If he trust to his own righteousness"

Ezekiel 33:13

Are you ready?

When we are tempted by Satan to commit a wrong act, our part is to exercise faith in the promises of God so that God can overcome the temptation *for us*. However, there is something that we do not want to do when we are tempted.

The rule holds true that, when we are dealing with God and His promises, "whatsoever is not of faith is sin" (Rom. 14:23). The reason that whatsoever is not of faith is sin is because unbelief in the Word of God is calling God a liar. "He that believeth not God hath made him a liar; because he believeth not the record that God gave" (1 John 5:10). Now since it is impossible for God to lie, when we call God a liar, *we are lying*. This is one reason why unbelief is sin.

Saving faith, as we learned earlier, is acknowledging the power of the Word of God to do the thing that it says, and to *depend upon that Word alone* to do it. "Whatsoever is not of faith is sin." When we plug the definition of saving faith into this passage, we have, "Whatsoever is not complete dependence upon the word of God to do what it says is sin." Here is where danger lies. Anything other than total dependence upon the Word of God to do what it says, to keep us from sinning, is sin. If you depend 99.99 percent upon the Word of God to do what it says, and yet depend upon anything else, even to the smallest degree, it is sin. If you depend upon the Word of God to keep you from sinning, and at the same time make personal, physical efforts to aid that word in doing what it says then you are not depending solely upon that Word *alone* to do it. Instead, you are depending partly upon what you can do. This is sin. The centurion manifested his faith by saying, "Speak the word *only.*" He recognized that the word *alone* was sufficient enough to do the thing that it said and that the words of Christ didn't need his help to do what they said. Our personal effort to help the Word of God to do what it says is an outward expression of inward unbelief. "*Whatsoever* is not of faith is sin."

Satan, when urging us to yield to temptation, would have us depend upon anything other than the Word of God for victory. The Word of God itself has the power to do the thing that it says without your physically needing to do anything. When we depend upon anything else other than the Word of God to do what the word says, it is sin. If we depend upon what we can or will do, it is sin. If we depend upon our ability to have devotions in the morning, to read our Bible, to pray, to walk away from the field of temptation, etc., if we depend upon any of these things, we are depending upon something other than the Word of God to keep us from sin. We are depending upon what *we* can do. This is not to say that we should not read our Bible and pray, for we must, but when we depend upon our ability to read and pray to

Chapter 7 — "If he trust to his own righteousness"

keep us from evil, then we are in error.

"God is righteous" (Dan. 9:14), and "God is love" (1 John 4:8). Therefore, righteousness is love, and love is a living, working, active principle. Love is not the law, "love is the *fulfilling* of the law" (Rom. 13:10). If love is not active in doing good for others, then it ceases to be love and becomes selfishness. Therefore, righteousness is right doing. Since righteousness is right doing, then self-righteousness would be the result of self's right-doing. So any effort of self to do right is a self-righteous effort. "All our righteousnesses are as filthy rags" (Isa. 64:6). The verse does not say, "all our righteousness *is* as filthy rags," but "all our righteousnesses *are* as filthy rags." Righteousnesses is plural, not singular. So all of our righteousnesses, right-doing's, are sin.

"Whatsoever is not of faith"—dependence upon the Word alone to do what it says—"is sin" (Rom. 14:23). If we depend upon anything other than the Word for our righteousness, for our right-doings, it is sin. Righteousness is *active. Righteousness is right doing*—it is a *verb*, not a noun. Therefore, when good works need to be done, when sin needs to be resisted, if we depend upon anything other than the Word to create that righteous action, it is sin.

The Lord of heaven declares, "When I shall say to the righteous, that he shall surely live; *if he trust to his own righteousness*, and commit iniquity, all his *righteousnesses* shall not be remembered; but for his iniquity that he hath committed, he shall die for it" (Eze. 33:13). To put this simply, if man trusts to his own right-doing, "he shall die for it," and "all his righteousnesses," right-doings, "shall not be remembered."

Self-dependence is the root of self-righteousness. A righteousness that is dependent upon the abilities and efforts of self, even in the smallest iota, is self-righteousness. The righteousness of God is not obtained through dependence upon self to do what it says. It is obtained by dependence upon the Word, by dependence upon the Author of that Word, that His Word alone will do what it says. Utter dependence upon the Word of God *is utter dependence upon the Word of God*. It requires no effort on your part to depend completely upon the Word to do everything for you. Those who strive to obtain righteousness by exerting every energy of their being, by their straining of every muscle, and their working of every nerve, are not depending *solely* upon the Word to do what it says, but to some degree, they are depending upon self and what self can do. And this is sin.

So what then is the effort? What is it that we are required to do if we expect to be saved? The people in Christ's time asked Him saying, "'What shall we do, that we might work the works of God?' . . . Their question meant, What shall we do that we may deserve heaven? What is the price we are required to pay in order to obtain the life to come?" (Ellen G. White, *The Desire of Ages*, p. 385). They wanted to know where their efforts were to be directed so that they might work God's works. Must they place their efforts toward obeying the rabbinical requirements, toward keeping the Ten Commandments, toward doing good deeds, or toward loving each other? Or perhaps it was their duty to be baptized as John, who had called them to repentance had directed. Jesus plainly answers their question and points out where their efforts are to be focused. "This is the work of God," He says, *"that ye believe"* (John 6:29).

And this is what it means to exercise saving faith in Jesus. It means

> *Self-dependence is the root of self-righteousness. A righteousness that is dependent upon the abilities and efforts of self, even in the smallest iota, is self-righteousness.*

Chapter 7 — "If he trust to his own righteousness"

to depend upon Him *alone*, the Word, to do what He says He will do. Dependence upon anything other than Jesus alone to save us from sin will result in self-righteousness, which is sin (Matt. 1:21).

This is the gospel of Jesus. It is *good news!* It is only in this message of righteousness by faith that the love of God can be seen most clearly"this do, and thou shalt live" (John 8:11; Luke 10:28). No, no! Rather, Jesus forgives our sins and then abides in our hearts, *living His life through us and overcoming sin for us.* Now that's love! Jesus died so that we might not have to die, but He has also given us His life so that we might really live. He wants us to take the gifts of His costly sacrifice just as they are, for free. It is true that salvation is *not* free, but it has been paid for.

> *Christ does not just merely forgive our sins and then coldly bid us, "go, and sin no more,"*

"Ask, and it shall be given you" (Matt. 7:7). "If ye shall ask any thing in my name, I will do it" (John 14:14). These words are the creative words of God. But there is a condition to this promise. "If we ask any thing *according to his will*, he heareth us" (1 John 5:14). While it is not for us to determine what God's will is outside of that which He has clearly revealed, we have the complete assurance that if we ask Him for something, and that something we ask for happens to fall within the domain of His good will, then since we believe, we have the gift we asked for. John continues the above verse, "And if we know that he hear us, whatsoever we ask, we *know* that we have the petitions that we desired of him" (verse 15).

We don't have to think, speculate, or reason because we *know* we *have* what we asked for, because our faith in the creative word of God causes that word to create for us the gift promised. God *said this*, and this is the strongest evidence that it is true. While we may not have the

Salvation Isn't Free... It's Been Paid For!

gift before we believe, we can know that the moment we believe that gift is created for us and is within our possession! It matters not what we feel or what emotions we experience, if we believe the promise, we have the gift!

Chapter 8

"Clean through the word"

John 15:3

Are you ready?

"Therefore we conclude that a man is justified by faith without the deeds of the law" (Rom. 3:28). "Therefore being justified by faith, we have peace with God through our Lord Jesus Christ" (Rom. 5:1). What does it mean to be justified? To be justified means to be made just. But what does it mean to be just?

When Christ was taken before Pilate to be judged, Pilate's wife, warned by God in a dream, sent a message to her husband saying, "Have thou nothing to do with that just man: for I have suffered many things this day in a dream because of him" (Matt. 27:19). Jesus was declared a just man, and upon inspection, Pilate could only say of Him, "I find in him no fault at all" (John 18:38). Jesus was and is "the Lamb of God, which taketh away the sin of the world" (John 1:29), "a lamb without blemish and without spot" (1 Peter 1:19). He "did no sin, neither was guile found in his mouth" (1 Peter 2:22). Jesus was a just man—a man without fault. Can a man be called a just man when he does unjustly? No. To be justified then means to be made without fault. When God justifies us, all of our guilt and sins are washed away, and all of our known character faults are destroyed. We are made perfect.

The Scriptures declare that we are justified *by faith*. And what is faith? Faith is depending upon the Word of God, that that Word *alone* will do what it says. We are justified then by depending upon the Word of Christ alone to justify us. No physical involvement is necessary for the Word to accomplish the thing that it says. The cleansing blood of Christ is applied to the soul when we depend upon the Word of God alone to apply it. And when we do this, instantly we are washed clean, and Jesus says to us, "Now ye are clean through the word which I have spoken unto you" (John 15:3).

But how shall a just man continue to live justly? How shall he continue to live without fault? "The just shall live by faith" (Heb. 10:38). How shall a just man live a blameless life? By faith, by depending upon the Word of God alone to do what it says. "Man shall not live by bread alone, but by every word that proceedeth out of the mouth of God" (Matt. 4:4). How shall a just man live without fault? A just man shall live faultlessly by depending upon every word that proceedeth out of the mouth of God, that that word alone will keep him from sinning.

This is sanctification. And how does the Bible say that men are sanctified? Paul's mission to the Gentiles was "to open their eyes, and to turn them from darkness to light, and from the power of Satan unto God, that they may receive forgiveness of sins, and inheritance among them which are *sanctified by faith* that is in me" (Acts 26:18). Sanctified by faith exercised in Christ; this is how man is sanctified.

"Sanctify them through thy truth: thy word is truth" (John 17:17). Jesus says that man is sanctified through the truth, and Jesus says that God's Word is truth. Therefore, we are sanctified by the Word. We are sanctified by depending upon the Word alone and trusting that the Word of God will sanctify us. But it is important to note that man is sanctified through truth. Lies have no power to sanctify because lies do not have creative power. The truth itself, because it is uttered from

Chapter 8 — "Clean through the word"

the mouth of God, has power in itself to sanctify us if we will but depend upon it alone to do what it says.

Jesus has paid the full price for our redemption, and oh what a price! The weight of one man's guilt is enough to crush out his life. But in order to give you the opportunity to be saved, Jesus suffered the guilt of *all* men. What a living nightmare! A *living* nightmare! For seemingly never-ending hours He bore this guilt on your behalf, not to mention the true death experience that He went through (Matt. 27:46). Why was there need for all of this suffering? Was it absolutely necessary? Yes. Jesus loved you enough that it was worth it to Him to bear the untold woe and to take the fearful risk.

Now what if Jesus had failed the test? What if he had failed His mission and fell to temptation in the wilderness? Remember, "the wages of sin is death" (Rom. 6:23). If Jesus had fallen to temptation and committed even a single sin during any point in His life, who would have been the Savior to deliver Him from the penalty of the law? Jesus risked His own eternal existence for us! And what shall be our response? Salvation is paid for, but it was *not* free. You can have it for free, but only because a very dear price was paid, only because the most extreme risk was made on your behalf. Is it that hard to choose to be a true Christian? Is it that hard to depend upon Jesus to do absolutely everything for you? Is it that hard to let Him live His life through you so that you can enjoy its blessings? What will you do? Decide now.

> *Jesus risked His own eternal existence for us! And what shall be our response? Salvation is paid for, but it was not free.*

Chapter 9

"By every word of God"

Luke 4:4

Are you ready?

"No man can serve two masters: for either he will hate the one, and love the other; or else he will hold to the one, and despise the other. Ye cannot serve God and mammon" (Matt. 6:24). Here Christ shows that it is not that man will not, or shall not serve two masters, but that he *cannot.* There is nothing more impossible than trying to serve both Christ and Satan at the same time. Jesus says, "He that is not with me *is against me*; and he that gathereth not with me *scattereth abroad*" (Matt. 12:30).

It is not necessary for one to deliberately choose to serve Satan to be on the side of evil. If you are not with Christ, if you do not purposefully choose to set yourself on His side, *you are* on the side of the wicked one. The flock that Christ is seeking to gather together, you are scattering abroad. There is no escaping this. There is no such thing as a fence-sitter. "For what fellowship hath righteousness with unrighteousness? and what

> *If you are not with Christ, if you do not purposefully choose to set yourself on His side, you are on the side of the wicked one.*

Chapter 9 — "By every word of God"

communion hath light with darkness? And what concord hath Christ with Belial? or what part hath he that believeth with an infidel? And what agreement hath the temple of God with idols?" (2 Cor. 6:14-16). There is no neutral in-between position. There is no compliance between good and evil, between Christ and Satan.

What does the word "therefore" mean? Let us use a familiar verse to illustrate its meaning. "Behold, I send you forth as sheep in the midst of wolves: be ye therefore wise as serpents, and harmless as doves" (Matt. 10:16). What does the word "therefore" mean in this verse? Jesus says that He sends us forth as sheep among wolves; *therefore* (since this is the case), we need to be as wise as serpents so that we aren't destroyed by the wolves, but we are still to remain as harmless as doves. The word "therefore" means that since such and such thing is the case, such and such must be done a certain way (or is a certain way). This is very basic and simple.

Now let us look at another point. "Behold, I send you forth as sheep in the midst of wolves: be ye therefore wise as serpents, and harmless as doves. But beware of men: for they will deliver you up to the councils, and they will scourge you in their synagogues; And ye shall be brought before governors and kings for my sake, for a testimony against them and the Gentiles. But when they deliver you up, *take no thought* how or what ye shall speak: for it shall be given you in that same hour what ye shall speak. For it is not ye that speak, but the Spirit of your Father which speaketh in you" (Matt. 10:16-20).

What do the words "take no thought" mean? What does Jesus mean when He says this? Christ means what He says. When Jesus says "take no thought," we are to understand Him to mean, "take no thought." In the original Greek, the words "take no thought" mean to not be anxious. Jesus is saying that even though you will be brought before governors and kings to give the reasons of your faith, do not even think about what you will say to them. There is no need to be anxious about it and to express that anxiety by taking thought about what you are going to say. But why not?

He continues, "For it shall be given you in that same hour what ye shall speak. For it is not ye that speak, but the Spirit of your Father which speaketh in you" (Matt. 10:19, 20). This is plain enough; there is no reason to mistake it. When we are brought before kings to answer for our faith, in that very hour, our Father in heaven will speak through us. This is the reason we are not to pre-think about what we are going to say. If we do pre-think about what we are going to say, it would be an outward expression of inward doubt; it would be doubting that our Father in heaven will give us the words to speak in the time of need. And "whatsoever is not of faith is sin" (Rom. 14:23).

Are you ready? Are you willing to accept truth? Will you reject truth because it does not harmonize with your opinions of what truth is? Will you allow your mind to be controlled by a cherished idea? Or will you accept truth regardless of feelings, regardless of consequences, and regardless of what your personal opinion is? Will you be swayed by the mind-controlling principles of the system of sin? Or will you stand abreast the storms of opposition and think for yourself? Make the decision right now to determine for yourself what truth is and take no man's say so. Man is not to think for you; you are to think for yourself. Do not trust the author of this book and take his word as truth. He is but man, *not God*. Be wise as a serpent. "Trust in the LORD with all thine heart; and *lean not unto*

> *Make the decision right now to determine for yourself what truth is and take no man's say so. Man is not to think for you; you are to think for yourself.*

Chapter 9 — "By every word of God"

thine own understanding. In all thy ways acknowledge him, and he shall direct thy paths. *Be not wise in thine own eyes"* (Prov. 3:5-7).

After declaring how perfectly impossible it is to serve God and Satan simultaneously, the very next word that Jesus utters is the word "therefore." Matthew 6:24 and 25 says, "No man can serve two masters: for either he will hate the one, and love the other; or else he will hold to the one, and despise the other. Ye cannot serve God and mammon. *Therefore* I say unto you, *Take no thought* for your life, what ye shall eat, or what ye shall drink; nor yet for your body, what ye shall put on" (Matt. 6:24, 25).

Jesus declares that since it is impossible to serve Him and Satan at the same time we are forbidden to take thought for our lives. Is Jesus plain enough? The instruction is "take no thought for your life." This is not a suggestion, it is a loving command, a blessed promise. When Jesus uses the word "therefore," He is saying that since you cannot serve God and mammon simultaneously, then, if you choose to serve God, you must not so much as even take thought for your own life as to how you will provide for yourself. Jesus makes it unmistakably clear that taking thought for our lives *is serving Satan*. And to take no thought means to *take no thought*.

And why shall we take no thought for our life? It is simple. Just like we are to take no thought for what we are going to say when we are brought before governors and kings to answer for our faith because God will give us what to speak, even so, God will provide for us when we are in need of food, water, and clothing. "Seek ye first the kingdom of God, and his righteousness; and all these things shall be added unto you" (Matt. 6:33).

"No man can serve two masters: for either he will hate the one, and love the other; or else he will hold to the one, and despise the other. Ye cannot serve God and mammon. Therefore I say unto you,

Take no thought for your life, what ye shall eat, or what ye shall drink; nor yet for your body, what ye shall put on. Is not the life more than meat, and the body than raiment? Behold the fowls of the air: for they sow not, neither do they reap, nor gather into barns; yet your heavenly Father feedeth them. Are ye not much better than they? Which of you by taking thought can add one cubit unto his stature?

"And why take ye thought for raiment? Consider the lilies of the field, how they grow; they toil not, neither do they spin: And yet I say unto you, That even Solomon in all his glory was not arrayed like one of these. Wherefore, if God so clothe the grass of the field, which to day is, and to morrow is cast into the oven, shall he not much more clothe you, O ye of little faith? *Therefore take no thought*, saying, What shall we eat? or, What shall we drink? or, Wherewithal shall we be clothed? (For after all these things do the Gentiles seek:) for *your heavenly Father knoweth that ye have need of all these things. But seek ye first the kingdom of God, and his righteousness; and all these things shall be added unto you. Take therefore no thought for the morrow: for the morrow shall take thought for the things of itself. Sufficient unto the day is the evil thereof'* (Matt. 6:24-34).

> *Shall we question the Word of God, which cannot lie? And to what avail would it be if we did? If we will only meet the two conditions of receiving the gift, the creative word will do what it says on our behalf.*

The Word of God is sufficient enough of itself to do the thing that it says without any physical involvement of ourselves to accomplish what it says. And what does the all-powerful creative word say here concerning our daily needs? It says plainly, "All these things shall be

Chapter 9 — "By every word of God"

added unto you." Shall we question the Word of God, which cannot lie? And to what avail would it be if we did? If we will only meet the two conditions of receiving the gift, the creative word will do what it says on our behalf.

But what are the conditions? "Seek ye first the kingdom of God, and his righteousness." Do these conditions to receiving our daily needs mention anything about planning out our lives, stressing ourselves over the matter, and going absolutely nuts trying to provide for ourselves the things that we need to sustain ourselves in this life? No. The Bible says to put God's kingdom and righteousness first in your life—to put them on the very top of your priority list—and actually take care of them *first*. If you do this, every provision necessary in this life will be provided for by the same word that spoke the universe into existence. The very promise itself has the power to provide for those who meet its conditions, and it does not need their help to fulfill itself to them.

Many Christians would say that this is an unbalanced teaching. Is it an unbalanced teaching? Maybe it is. Find out for yourself. Would Jesus teach an unbalanced doctrine? Jesus is no fanatic, and neither is He a fool. Christ means what He says.

"Let no man deceive himself. If any man among you seemeth to be wise in this world, let him become a fool, that he may be wise. For the wisdom of this world is foolishness with God" (1 Cor. 3:18, 19). The worldly wisdom of fools is that which would take the words of Jesus and make them to mean what they do not. Methods, traditions, customs, habits and practices—in all their forms—should not be allowed to reshape the Word of God in the minds of men. Many would insist that we must do more than seek first God's kingdom and righteousness to receive that provision necessary for life because this is the way that it has always been, and to these Christ says, "Full well ye reject the commandment of God, that ye may keep your own tradition" (Mark 7:9).

Do men say that we need to be careful when it comes to providing for our daily needs? Then let them hear the words of Scripture, "Be careful for nothing" (Phil. 4:6). The word careful here means to be anxious about and to take thought. The literal breakdown of the word is careful, meaning, full of care. So then we are to be anxious about nothing, to take thought for nothing, and to be full of care for nothing. How can we fully let go and follow this principle? "Be careful for nothing; but in every thing by prayer and supplication with thanksgiving let your requests be made known unto God." We are to be careful for nothing because we know that we can request of God those things that we need, and we shall receive them according to His will.

Christ is not willing for us to be anxious about how we are going to have our daily needs supplied because He knows that this is serving Satan. It is unbelief in our Father's care that He will provide for us those things that we need. In the parable of the sower, Jesus listed "the cares of this world" (Mark 4:19) as one of those primary things that keep men from receiving the free gift of salvation. "Seek ye first the kingdom of God, and his righteousness; and all these things *shall be added unto you*" (Matt. 6:33). Anything more or anything less than these plainest of words is a lie devised by the spirit of Satan to destroy the human race.

This is not to say that man is to be idle and indolent. After the fall of Adam and Eve, God said to Adam, "cursed is the ground *for thy sake*; in sorrow shalt thou eat of it all the days of thy life; Thorns also and thistles shall it bring forth to thee; and thou shalt eat the herb of the field; In the sweat of thy face shalt thou eat bread, till thou return unto the ground; for out of it wast thou taken: for dust thou art, and unto dust shalt thou return" (Gen. 3:17-19). God cursed the ground for

Chapter 9 — "By every word of God"

man's sake. God appointed labor to humanity as a means of blessing, to occupy his time in useful work that would uplift his character and foster in him responsibility and diligence. But the blessing of labor *is not* to be understood as the source of our daily provision.

But since we must labor, let us look at it in the light that God gives it. "Six days *shalt thou* labour, and do all thy work" (Ex. 20:9). This command is a promise. God is promising you that you will labor and will thus receive all the blessings that come with it. This promise of God alone is sufficient enough of itself to cause you to labor. Just depend upon that word to do what it says. Do not worry about the physical exertion necessary for you to labor all of those six days. The Word of God itself is sufficient enough to do what it says without any physical involvement of yours necessary to accomplish what it says. Just depend upon that Word to do what it says, knowing that it will do it since it cannot possibly lie because of its creative power, and doing this, *it is done*. Relax, and let the creative word of God exert energy for you.

"Man shall not live by bread alone, but by every word that proceedeth out of the mouth of God" (Matt. 4:4). How is man to live? By every word that comes from the mouth of God. Man is to live by depending upon every word that proceeds out of the mouth of God, that that word itself will do what it says. And what does that word say it will do? "Seek ye first the kingdom of God, and his righteousness; *and all these things shall be added unto you*" (Matt. 6:33). Depend upon the Word alone, that it will do what it says, know that it is done, and all these things *are* added unto you. The Lord of heaven has spoken. Let us not question Him. Rather, let us question the words of so often misinformed and strongly opinionated finite men whose wisdom God declares as foolishness.

How was ancient Israel provided for during their forty years in the wilderness? "Thou shalt remember all the way which the LORD thy God led thee these forty years in the wilderness, to humble thee, and to prove thee, to know what was in thine heart, whether thou wouldest keep his commandments, or no. And he humbled thee, and suffered thee to hunger, and fed thee with manna, which thou knewest not, neither did thy fathers know; that he might make thee know that man doth not live by bread only, but by every word that proceedeth out of the mouth of the LORD doth man live. Thy raiment waxed not old upon thee, neither did thy foot swell, these forty years" (Deut. 8:2-4).

> *It was God's design to teach them that man lived, not by human effort, not by labor, not by any devising of man, but that they lived and found provision for their daily needs in every word that proceeded out of the mouth of God.*

In providing manna for the children of Israel during their forty-year wilderness experience, it was God's design to teach them that man lived, not by human effort, not by labor, not by any devising of man, but that they lived and found provision for their daily needs in every word that proceeded out of the mouth of God. And shall we forget this lesson? Shall the opinions of foolish men cause us to forget the very truth that will help us to better understand the love of God for us? Shall the mind-controlling principles of the machine turn us from our allegiance to the altogether lovely King of the universe? Will it turn us from our loving Father in heaven?

But what happens when we suffer a little hardship in serving Christ. What then? The Lord says, "Be still, and know that I am God"

Chapter 9 — "By every word of God"

(Ps. 46:10). "We brought nothing into this world, and it is certain we can carry nothing out. And having food and raiment let us be therewith content" (1 Tim. 6:7, 8). For "we know that all things work together for good to them that love God" (Rom. 8:28), "for he doth not afflict willingly nor grieve the children of men" (Lam. 3:33), "for all things are for your sakes" (2 Cor. 4:15) "that we might be partakers of his holiness"(Heb 12:10).

Chapter 10

"Taken in the devices"

Psalms 10:2

`Are you ready?

The machine—mindless, cold, heartless, and wicked beyond all imagination—is destroying the minds and bodies of millions of people. As a red-eyed, forked-tongued dragon, the machine reveals itself, but only in the guise of an innocent newborn. With its metallic, cord-like tentacles fastened on the heads of its victims, it sucks the life out of them, controlling their minds and using them as a means of fastening others in its death grip and wrapping them up in the system of sin. Its victims are asleep; they are in a dream world. They are not aware that they are cocooned in the spider's web, for it has taken away their ability to reason. They are doped up with poison. The machine has programmed them to believe whatever it says. It thinks for them and they can do nothing but obey.

The machine controls us and dominates our minds by wrapping us up in the things of this world.

Chapter 10 — "Taken in the devices"

It receives its sustenance *only* as its victims feed upon its lies. Should every soul on earth cease to believe the lying falsehoods it utters, the machine would be instantly blotted out of existence.

There is no hope for a victim of the machine, so long as its grasp on them is tight. There is no outsider who can wrench a victim from the machine's grasp, or even so much as loosen its grip. The only way a victim of the machine can be set free from its nasty jaws is if the mind-controlled individual chooses to be set free from it by believing truth and denying lies. The reason that this is nearly impossible is because the machine controls their minds. It has brainwashed them into thinking that they are free and that their minds are not being controlled by anything. It has programmed them to believe that they are thinking individuals that both think and reason for themselves, and that they in fact believe truth. But the victims cannot see that this is not the case. Their very thoughts are guided by the machine. They have been trained to think and reason like the machine would have them think and reason, and they can do nothing else. And so what hope is there?

Who wrote the blueprints for this vicious monster? Who put it together? What is its end purpose? When will it be destroyed? How can it be unplugged? And why must I be involved in frying its circuitry?

Are you ready? Once you read this chapter, there is no turning back. If you turn back after reading this chapter, if you close your eyes and ears and turn your head, you are making a choice that will assure yourself a place among the lost until the time of your repentance, if you ever do repent. My question to you is, *are you ready?*

That great mastermind of evil, the one who is altogether wicked, is the one who made the blueprints for the machine. Working through the minds of his devoted subjects, the devil has put together and set in motion a system of life, the system of sin, whose end purpose is to malign, torture, and destroy. Its purpose is to make miserable everything in existence for as long as it possibly can.

Before a child is ever born, the machine spreads its nasty lies about for the express purpose of maligning the innocent babe's happiness. The parents of the child believe everything the machine has taught them and because of this they are weighed down with continual burdens and sorrow. One in spirit or divided, they are constantly falling to temptation. The parents find themselves stuck in life and in their relationship, unnecessarily fighting and arguing. They cannot find a way out of their problems, because the machine's lies, which it has propagated as truth, are the way of life for the couple. In their minds there is no other way to live. Lack of funds or the abundance therefore, lack or abundance of time and attention for each other, and the many differing opinions and choices of the husband and wife, with all of the problems that they so often cause, are the conditions under which a child is brought into existence; that is, if the conditions are even that favorable.

The pre-prescribed blueprint for the innocent babe's life, character, and happiness is the miserable existence of its parents. The machine would have it no other way, for that is the only way to assure its continued presence in this world. The child lives and grows, wanting only to die. It cannot help but believe every lie that the machine establishes in its mind because those lies are presented as the purest of truths to the child. The child then accepts these false truths and is led subconsciously to understand that truth is saddening and leads to misery while falsehoods and lies lead to happiness. The child then either chooses a seemingly easier way out of his misery through premature death or drugs or continues to live the miserable life that the machine desires.

Whether Christian or agnostic, atheist or believer, as the child

Chapter 10 — "Taken in the devices"

grows, he becomes more and more part of the machine. Just another part added to it to propagate its lies and provide for its continued existence. He is just another brick in the wall to defend the machine against its remnant enemies—those who obey God and follow His commandments. His thoughts are controlled, or at least molded by the machine. It programs him well to think himself wise when he is a fool. It educates him to be faithful in remaining its wonderfully supportive mind slave.

When the opportunity presents itself to the new member of society to help those who have been afflicted by the system of sin, the machine shows them that if they help the poor and misfortunate that they themselves will come to want. The machine tells them to shut their ears and cover their eyes from seeing and hearing the needs of the poor. It tells them to turn their heads in another direction, lest they also become poor and needy. Thus millions upon millions of dying souls are turned away from, their needs ignored, and their souls left to be plundered by the devil.

To all of these slaves of the machine whom it causes to turn away, Jesus will say in the day of final judgment, "Depart from me, ye cursed, into everlasting fire, prepared for the devil and his angels: For I was an hungred, and ye gave me no meat: I was thirsty, and ye gave me no drink: I was a stranger, and ye took me not in: naked, and ye clothed me not: sick, and in prison, and ye visited me not" (Matt. 25:41-43). And the servants

But the great Searcher of hearts will answer them with words that burn their souls like scorching coals of fire, "Verily I say unto you, Inasmuch as ye did it not to one of the least of these, ye did it not to me"

of the machine shall respond to Him saying, "Lord, when saw we thee an hungred, or athirst, or a stranger, or naked, or sick, or in prison, and did not minister unto thee?" (verse 44). But the great Searcher of hearts will answer them with words that burn their souls like scorching coals of fire, "Verily I say unto you, Inasmuch as ye did it not to one of the least of these, ye did it not to me" (verse 45). They knew to do good, but they did it not, and to them "it is sin" (James 4:17).

Thus the word of the Lord will again hold true as He gave us through kings Solomon and David: "Whoso stoppeth his ears at the cry of the poor, he also shall cry himself, but shall not be heard" (Prov. 21:13)."He that giveth unto the poor shall not lack: but he that hideth his eyes shall have many a curse" (Prov. 28:27). "The righteous considereth the cause of the poor: but the wicked regardeth not to know it" (Prov. 29:7). "The wicked in his pride doth persecute the poor: let them be taken in the devices that they have imagined" (Ps. 10:2). The poor in these verses is not merely referring to those who don't have money. It refers to those who are in need physically, mentally, emotionally, and spiritually. The poor then includes the entire human race. The wicked are said to persecute these needy ones, and the psalmist prays, "let them be taken in the devices that they have imagined."

The word "devices" in its singular form, in the original Greek means, machination. Machination is an evil plot, an evil plan to accomplish wicked ends. Man, inspired by the very spirit of Satan, has created a machine for the purpose of evil. By their machination they "grind the faces of the poor" (Isa. 3:15) that they might be increased and not be interrupted from rising higher in the scale of "good living." But the prayer of the psalmist has been answered, and man is now controlled by the machine that he has created. The machine has developed a mind and life of its own, and man has been taken by his

Chapter 10 — "Taken in the devices"

own evil plot. "He that oppresseth the poor to increase his riches, and he that giveth to the rich, shall surely come to want" (Prov. 22:16). "The turning away of the simple shall slay them, and the prosperity of fools shall destroy them" (Prov. 1:32).

But suppose that one did see it a duty to help those in need. Suppose that he was not so brainwashed by the machine that he could actually perceive that not helping to save those who are dying is to be guilty of murdering them. Suppose that his heart goes out in sympathy for them and he is roused to do something to help. How shall he overcome the temptation to close his eyes and ears and turn his head away from the needy? When the life-sucking monster tells him that he must not help those in need, and that he must instead continue in the system to be able to provide for his own needs, how shall he gain victory over the sin of indifference? The machine teaches him that he must do more than seek first God's kingdom and righteousness to be able to live himself, much less to be able to help others. What shall he do? How can he stand against such imperceptible lies and give away to those in need when by doing so he shall come to want himself? He shall stand and overcome by the power of the Word—the creative power of truth.

> *But the prayer of the psalmist has been answered, and man is now controlled by the machine that he has created.*

King Solomon wrote, "There is that maketh himself rich, yet hath nothing: there is that maketh himself poor, yet hath great riches" (Prov. 13:7). "There is that scattereth, and yet increaseth; and there is that withholdeth more than is meet, but it tendeth to poverty" (Prov. 11:24). *"Give, and it shall be given unto you,"* says Jesus, "good measure, pressed down, and shaken together, and running over, shall men give into your bosom. For with the same measure that ye mete withal *it shall be measured to you again*" (Luke 6:38).

Jesus is either a liar or He is not. His word either has creative power of itself to do what it says, or it does not. Jesus says that if you seek first God's kingdom and righteousness before everything else the creative word of God will add unto you all the things you need in order to live in this world and that there will be enough to give to others in need. Jesus' creative word says that if you give, "*it shall be given unto you.*" The machine teaches that Jesus is a liar and that it is not enough to seek God's kingdom and righteousness first to receive everything you need for this life. It teaches that you must follow in the path that it has laid out to be successful and that anything short of this leads to certain ruin. It teaches that if you give, you shall come to want. It doesn't mind if you keep your religion, but you cannot help those in need, because if you do you will not be able to make it yourself. You cannot rise up and forsake all to save those who are dying, or you yourself will die. The machine teaches that man shall not live by every creative word that proceeds out of the mouth of God, but that he shall live by a bread of his own worried and feeble efforts.

Thus the machine has proven itself responsible for the great delay in the preaching of the gospel. It is responsible for the loss of millions of souls who have died without hope, without a Savior! It controls the minds of many so that they will not accept the truth, so that they will not accept the gospel. It is responsible for leading them to commit the unpardonable sin! It is responsible for the starvation of millions and millions of innocent children. But is it the machine that is responsible for the world's suffering and misery? Or is it those who have supported this nasty beast by believing and promoting its lies? It is the latter. While men may have been deceived into believing a lie and thus allowing to perish multitudes of unsaved souls, when the

Chapter 10 — "Taken in the devices"

light comes to them that they are guilty of believing and loving the lies of Satan and they choose not to change, God no longer winks at the time of their ignorance. "If I had not come and spoken unto them, they had not had sin: *but now they have no cloak for their sin*" (John 15:22).

There is no excuse that can be made. All of the endless provisions of heaven are pledged on our behalf to use for the good of others. How wonderful it is! We are perfectly free to heal the wounds and relieve the pain of the sorrowing and afflicted around the globe. There are no cares of this world to bind us down and keep us from sharing the gospel. Those who are controlled by the machine can break free through the power of God. There is nothing that can keep us from giving bread to the hungry, water to the thirsty, and clothes to the naked. With Christ as our Husband, our relationship has placed us in possession of all of the limitless resources of Jehovah. We are literally in part-ownership of all created things. We are not in control of them all, but as we have need from our Husband and ask Him in faith, then according to our faith *it is unto us!* God cannot lie. It is impossible. His word has creative power to do what it says. His word is true. Says the Lord, "All the earth is mine" (Ex. 19:5). Therefore, "Ask, and it shall be given you" (Matt. 7:7), for "if we ask any thing according to his will, he heareth us" (1 John 5:14). "According to your faith *be it unto you*" (Matt. 9:29). And "believing, *ye shall receive*" (Matt. 21:22).

> *All of the endless provisions of heaven are pledged on our behalf to use for the good of others.*

No longer must there be a continual turning away from the poor and needy. No longer do they have to be dragged down by the stone and drowned in their sins. They can be set free in Christ if you will just choose to believe and love the truth and share it to the world. It requires no more, and it requires no less. Just exercise faith by depending upon the Word of God *alone*, that that Word will, *of itself*, do the things that it says. It is all within your reach to make a mighty change for good in this world and break the chains of the machine. *It's time to make a difference!* God calls, as His followers, to actively help those around us, thus saving them from the powers of Satan and a society that is caught within the snare of the machine. Proverbs 14:21 says, "He that hath mercy on the poor, *happy is he*." Furthermore, the creative word of God also says, "Blessed is he that considereth the poor: the LORD *will deliver him* in time of trouble" (Ps. 41:1).

Chapter 11

"What to do with purple bunnies"

2 James 18:25

Are you ready?
What shall we do with purple bunnies? So many people are always found asking the wrong questions. "How can I overcome temptation?" they ask. When people ask themselves this question, they are automatically assuming that it is something that *they* can do. This is the problem. We do not understand that we cannot possibly overcome temptation. Yes, temptation can be overcome, but *we* cannot overcome it. The Word of God itself is able to do what it says without any physical involvement from us necessary to accomplish what it says, namely, to keep us from sinning. The Word of God itself overcomes the temptation on our behalf. We are to be "*kept by the power of God* through faith [dependence upon the Word of God *alone*, that the Word will do what it says] unto salvation" (1 Peter 1:5).

Another wrong question that we often ask ourselves is, "How will *I* be able to provide for myself?" It is true that we can be provided for, but can *we* provide for ourselves? "And he [the Lord] humbled thee, and suffered thee to hunger, and fed thee with manna, which thou knewest not, neither did thy fathers know; that he might make thee know that man doth not live by bread only, but by every word that proceedeth out of the mouth of the LORD doth man live" (Deut. 8:3).

Bread alone is not sufficient enough for man to be able to live. Man is enabled to live by every life-giving, creative word that comes from the mouth of God. Bread itself cannot make the heart beat, the lungs expand, or the brain function. Bread cannot even exist without the creative word of God causing the sun to shine, the rain to fall, and the wheat to grow. The sun, the rain, the wheat, and even man himself, are "kept in store," preserved, "by the same word" that brought them all into existence (2 Peter 3:7). That same creative word promises to provide everything we need. So to answer our question, *we are not* able to provide for our existence. The life-giving word of God is the only thing that can sustain and provide for our life.

Do you see how asking the wrong questions can lead us into misery? The machine has taught us to ask the wrong questions, and this is why we so often suffer under such a load of care and guilt. But what about purple bunnies?

Do purple bunnies exist? No, they do not. So the question, "What shall we do with purple bunnies?" is the wrong question. If purple bunnies do not exist, we do not need to do anything with them, because they aren't there. But many people are affected by purple bunnies because they wonder what they are going to do with them.

What is a lie? What is the purpose of a lie? If someone lied to you saying that at this very moment there was a purple bunny in your shoe nibbling on your sock and that you better do something about it before matters got worse, what is the purpose of the lie? In reality, the purple bunny does not exist, it is not in your shoe, and it is not nibbling on your sock. But the lie sought to establish in your mind that there really is a purple bunny in your shoe nibbling on your sock. Again, in reality the purple bunny does not exist. But if you believe the lie, the purple bunny *does exist, but only in your mind.*

Lies exist *only* in the minds of those who believe them. Outside of

Chapter 11 — "What to do with purple bunnies"

that, lies are fake. They are not real, and they do not exist. *The lie itself exists* because there are such things as lies, but that thing that the lie is trying to establish does *not* exist, *except in the minds of those who believe the lie.* Now, if something does not exist, shall we allow it to affect our lives and hold us as prisoners?

Satan continually lies to us by his insinuated thoughts and feelings, which come to us in the form of temptations, but shall that which does not exist affect our lives? His temptations are just *lies*, they do *not* exist. His temptations are nothing more than purple bunnies, and why shall we allow them to destroy our peace and happiness? Shall we respond to those things that do not exist and thus bring damnation upon ourselves and others? No! That would be foolish. Satan's temptations are a form of mind control, which we must resist at all costs. Satan tries to snare us in the machine and its false way of life. The lie that the machine is seeking to establish in the minds of people is that if you plug yourself into it you will end up an educated person living a good life. But the good life and true education that Satan presents, in all reality, *does not exist.* So if it does not exist, why do some people devote their lives to obtaining the unattainable? *They do not exist!* They are nothing but purple bunnies.

The machine has a system set in place to sustain its life. Its networks of lies encircle the entire planet. The educational systems of the day, the appointed way to make a living in today's world, the "educated" men who pass its lies down along the line, these are the machine's tangible tools. But the machine itself, while so alive and real, while so effective to control the minds and lives of many men, does not exist, because it is a lie. It is a lie that lies.

The machine is seen as its manipulative mind-controlling principles are exercised to take away the ability of its prey to think and reason for itself. This is the machine at work. Here it is made visible. But its workings are the workings of lies, and they therefore don't exist. *The lies themselves exist*, but what they are trying to establish in the minds of men *do not exist*, except in the minds of those who believe the lies. Thus, the machine exists because there are such things as lies, and yet it doesn't exist because its lies, its workings, are only imaginary. And only as the lies, the imaginary things, are accepted and believed by the machine's prey, do they exist and have power to steal away the minds of men and make them the slaves of sin.

The machine's chief objective is to take away our freedoms—but we must fight back. We are in a battle in which there can be no neutrality. You either feed, nourish, and protect this beastly tyrant, or you starve it to death. You don't have to choose one side or the other to be on one of them. By indecision you are just as surely on the machine's side as if you purposefully and wholeheartedly joined it by choice.

"*No man can serve two masters*: for either he will hate the one, and love the other; or else he will hold to the one, and despise the other. Ye *cannot* serve God and mammon. Therefore I say unto you, *Take no thought for your life*, what ye shall eat, or what ye shall drink; nor yet for your body, what ye shall put on . . . But *seek ye first the kingdom of God, and his righteousness*; and all these things shall be added unto you" (Matt. 6:24, 25, 33).

You can either serve the machine, or you can serve Christ. It is impossible to serve them both. They are two completely antagonistic parties. You can either obey the machine by taking thought for your life, or you can obey Christ by taking no thought for your life. You can either choose to believe and love lies, or you can choose to believe and love truth. It is your choice. There is no compulsion exerted. If you must, for whatever reason, have anything to do with the machine other than destroying it, *use it,* but *never* let it use you.

Chapter 11 — "What to do with purple bunnies"

Freedom of thought and conscience; freedom of choice, action, and reason; *freedom to be free*—what will you do without these freedoms? Think about it! What will you do without freedom? Will you live as a captive to be slain by the captor? Why not fight for freedom and eternal life? Will you fight to free others? Will you fight to free the poor slaves of the machine before it hurls them into eternity, destitute of a Savior? In fighting, you may very well die, but if you don't fight, yes you may live a little longer in this world, but you will have no part in the world to come. It is better to die free than to live a slave, just to die in the end anyway.

Should you forget the question to every answer, the effect to every cause, and the solution to every problem, remember this one question and determine the answer for yourself. Will I allow purple bunnies to ruin my life and destroy the lives of others?

The Scriptures declare that there is "a time to kill" and "a time to hate" (Eccl. 3:3, 8). Therefore, there must be something worthy of hating and killing. The time to hate is *now*, and the thing to hate is the machine. Let us smash this miserable thing to pieces. Lies are the cause of all of the suffering in the universe. The machine is one of the biggest and grossest liars in existence. Its sole goal is to hold as many victims as it can in its death grip so that when the fires of hell come to consume it, its prey will not be able to escape. The machine is going down, and it wants to take everyone with it. It is seeking to destroy the people you love, your family and friends. Yes, in many cases, it is already destroying them. Wreck havoc on the wretched thing! Show it no mercy, for it will show you none in return.

> *It is better to die free than to live a slave, just to die in the end anyway.*

Salvation Isn't Free... It's Been Paid For!

Let us now stand for truth in defiance of tyranny. Let us boldly rebel against that old serpent. We owe him no allegiance, nor have we ever, for he is not our God, nor will he ever be. Let us turn square about and face this vicious monster. The machine may very well rob us of our lives, but it shall *never* steal away our freedoms. Let us inform our conceited enemy that his plans are foiled, that the battle is the Lord's, that we choose to believe the truth, and that we shall win this war! That which is "quick, and powerful, and sharper than any twoedged sword," the power of the Word—Jesus—is on our side, and He will win (Heb. 4:12).

> *Let us inform our conceited enemy that his plans are foiled, that the battle is the Lord's, that we choose to believe the truth, and that we shall win this war!*

Therefore, "ye shall not need to fight in this battle: set yourselves, stand ye still, and see the salvation of the LORD . . . go out against them: for the LORD will be with you" (2 Chron. 20:17). "Ye shall not fear them: for the LORD your God he shall fight for you" (Deut. 3:22), "and ye shall hold your peace" (Ex. 14:14). "Thus saith the LORD . . . *I will contend with him that contendeth with thee.* (Isa. 49:25).

Are you ready *for battle*? "This is the condemnation, that light is come into the world, and men loved darkness rather than light" (John 3:19). "For this cause God shall send them strong delusion, that they should believe a lie: That they all might be damned who believed not the truth, but had pleasure in unrighteousness" (2 Thess. 2:11, 12). "If I had not come and spoken unto them, they had not had sin: but now they have no cloak for their sin" (John 15:22). "If it seem evil unto you to serve the LORD, choose you this day whom ye will serve" (Joshua

Chapter 11 — "What to do with purple bunnies"

24:15). "I call heaven and earth to record this day against you, that I have set before you life and death, blessing and cursing: therefore *choose life*, that both thou and thy seed may live" (Deuteronomy 30:19).

Salvation Isn't Free… It's Been Paid For!

What To Do With Purple Bunnies

Oh what shall I do?
Purple bunny is in my shoe
This must be just a dream
But the bunny has no seam

Purple bunny's fluffy tail
Went outside to get the mail
Oh how useful of all things
Wish that bunny had some wings

I've got to get to work
But this bunny is a quirk
She's broken my new clock
And she's nibbling on my sock

Munching on a carrot
This bunny is no parrot
But oh what shall I do
Purple bunny is in my shoe

I pray she doesn't die
Even though she is a lie
She's the cutest of all things
But boy she's got some fangs

Chapter 11 — "What to do with purple bunnies"

Hopping all around
This bunny must be bound
Give me back my shoe!
Purple bunny I've got you

But now how shall I stand
Purple bunny is in my hand
Look her in the eyes
There only full of lies

But now what shall I do?
Shall I put her in my shoe?
Conscience says, "Do not!
Rather put her in the pot."

I go and grab the pot
Then I find the bunny is not
Now I've got my perfect sock
And my new unbroken clock

But now what shall you do?
Purple bunny is in your shoe
Now the bunny is in your hand
And oh how shall you stand?

Salvation Isn't Free… It's Been Paid For!

Break the Machine

Trained to be idiots
Told that they'll be wise
Taught to be foolish
It's wearing a disguise

"You'll get an education!"
Is its favorite phrase
Oh tell me what's the problem?
You must be in a daze

Programmed to be mindless
Told what to believe
Forced into submission
Its purpose to deceive

Mind-controlling garbage
The stupid wicked thing
The life sucking leecher
It's just a dumb machine

Chapter 11 — "What to do with purple bunnies"

The greater is their sorrow
The more may be your glee
But wait till it's all over
You're pain will finest be

I promise that I'll kill you
As far as humans can
You'll burn in hell forever
If you touch them once again

There is no turning back now
"I'm done!" I said, "I'm done!"
So kiss good-bye the victory
Cuz it's already won

Chapter 12

Are you ready?

Now you're ready!

The word of God is sufficient enough *of itself* to do what it says without any physical involvement from you necessary to accomplish what it says. And what does the Word say? The Word says, "Thy sins be forgiven thee" (Mark 2:5). This word is sufficient enough. You *are* forgiven since you are taking Christ at His word and are depending upon Him to forgive you. It's so simple! And what else does the Word say? It says, "Go, and sin no more" (John 8:11). Since you are depending upon that Word *alone,* that it will do what it says, you will be kept safe from all temptation to sin, *as long as you continue to depend upon the Word.* Here is salvation, full, complete, and oh so wonderfully free! You can have it for free, but only because it has been paid for.

What else does the Word say? It says, "Seek ye first the kingdom of God, and his righteousness; and all these things shall be added unto you" (Matt. 6:33). This word *alone* is sufficient enough to provide everything necessary for you to be able to live successfully in this world. Depend upon it, and all its limitless provisions are yours. You are now set free from worldly cares so that you can fulfill the gospel commission. "Go ye therefore, and teach all nations" (Matt. 28:19). What shall you teach them? You shall teach them truth. You must not make them believe truth; they must see it for themselves and

Chapter 12 — Are you ready?

be grounded in it. If you use mind-controlling principles on them to manipulate them into believing what you do, then they will not be able to withstand the storm, and you will only be helping the machine to destroy them.

As those you teach accept the truth and know it for themselves, they will be set free from the power of sin; they will be set free from the machine. And freed from Satan's grasp, they will join the arising army to finish preaching the gospel. And when "this gospel of the kingdom shall be preached in all the world for a witness unto all nations . . . then shall the end come" (Matt. 24:14).

Let us now be free from purple bunnies, let us be free from the machine, let us be free from sin, and let us be happy. Let us love and depend upon Jesus, let us kill the machine, and let us go home. Amen.

We invite you to view the complete
selection of titles we publish at:

www.TEACHServices.com

or write or email us your praises,
reactions, or thoughts about this
or any other book we publish at:

TEACH Services, Inc.
P.O. Box 954
Ringgold, GA 30736

info@TEACHServices.com

Finally, if you are interested in seeing
your own book in print, please contact us at

publishing@teachservices.com.

We would be happy to review your manuscript for free.

www.ingramcontent.com/pod-product-compliance
Lightning Source LLC
Chambersburg PA
CBHW070053120426
42742CB00048B/2510